THE
UX LEARNER'S GUIDEBOOK

A Ramp and Reference for Aspiring UX Designers

Chad Camara
Yujia Zhao

ISBN-13: 978-0996399807 (Deuxtopia, Inc.)
ISBN-10: 0996399801

To all the great designers, researchers, programmers, product managers, friends, and teachers we have worked with.

Thank You

Contents

Introduction

The field of User Experience Design is currently enjoying a kind of "chic mystique", garnering interest from many people wanting to understand UX Design and how to get into the field. As UX professionals we frequently receive UX Design inquiries from people all around the world, from students trying to decide on a profession, to graphic designers and UI developers looking to make a change, to current UX professionals seeking to learn more.

And for good reason. UX Design is a pretty fun job. UX Designers rarely have a boring or predictable day, as there are always problems to be solved and creative work to be done. At its most pure, it is a profession that seeks to enact positive change in the world. UX Designers aim to make technology more accessible, engaging, and intuitive for people. It is very rewarding to see someone excited to use a product that you worked on, and you can watch as that product positively affects their life in some way. Also, it surely doesn't hurt that UX Design is an in-demand job with pretty good compensation.

We are excited to share our knowledge when we get questions about UX Design, but we often find the limited words of an email or instant message exchange are not nearly enough to communicate how to get educated, get a job, and continue growing as a UX professional.

This book is our answer to everyone who wants to know:

> What is User Experience?
> How do I get into the User Experience Field?
> What does a User Experience Designer do?
> What skills are required to be a User Experience Designer?
> What should I do to learn User Experience Design?
> How can I become a better User Experience Designer?

The Elusive Field

Looking back at our own individual journeys to become UX professionals we realized that User Experience Design is an exciting and challenging profession, but it is an elusive one as well. The field is still relatively new, and any discipline at this young stage experiences growing pains as it figures itself out on the fly. Companies and industry experts refer to UX by many different names and place UX in a variety of departments. Inside of companies UX is typically part of product development but sometimes it is considered part of engineering or even marketing. And the actual work that UX Designers do still varies drastically from job to job.

Doctors go to medical school, lawyers go to law school, and chefs go to culinary school. Programmers and computer engineers have a variety of computer science degrees available at nearly every college in the world. But for UX Design, there isn't a standard "UX school", nor is there even close to a commonly agreed-upon curriculum for teaching UX Design. Every year there are always another couple of schools that offer courses related to UX, and there are some great schools that teach interaction design, product design, human factors, and human-computer interaction. But there still isn't a specific curriculum for becoming a "UX Designer", and that is what we aim to address with this book.

We have benefitted from a great formal education in HCI/d from Indiana University, as well as a very wide range of working experience. We have continued to learn on the job alongside numerous talented UX researchers and designers. Between the two of us we have worked for over 10 companies on an array of products from enterprise software to consumer applications and hardware. We have worked for large established companies, startups, and design consultancies. We have worked in full-time, freelance, and part-time roles. We even design and develop products on our own from time to time.

Our combination of formal education, diverse real-world experience, and self-study has given us a broad perspective on UX Design. We have also spent a lot of time reflecting on our own growth as we have helped mentor others in their own design careers. Through all of this we know that it starts with developing a strong, comprehensive foundation of knowledge, skills, tools, and personal design philosophy in order to produce good work and grow as a UX Designer.

Who is this book for?

This book is intended for anyone who is serious about understanding what it takes to become a User Experience Designer. This includes:

- Students who want to pursue a career in User Experience Design or related fields

- User Experience Designers looking for a refresher or a new perspective on the field

- Anyone in the technology industry who wants to take on User Experience Design responsibilities within their product organization, such as software developers, graphic designers, or product managers

- Managers or other product leaders who want to kickstart their own understanding or teach their teams about User Experience Design

Becoming a UX Designer – Foundations

Drawing from our own expertise and experience, this book offers that strong foundation for people who aspire to become UX Designers. While there are books, blogs, online courses, and websites about UX Design, it is very hard to know where to begin, especially with what makes sense for someone just starting out. In our own UX career path we have often been frustrated at how broad and disorganized much of the information about the UX field is.

With this book we want to provide a reference guide of the essentials for aspiring UX Designers:

Chapter 1 · UX Overview
What is UX Design and what does a UX Designer do?

Chapter 2 · Learning Advice
Best practices for learning UX Design

Chapter 3 · The Design Process
How UX Design happens

Chapter 4 · Research & Design Methods
Fundamental design methods and tools to be familiar with

Chapter 5 · UX Design Competency
The collection of knowledge and skills that make a designer

Chapter 6 · Jobs
Practical advice on how to get a job as a UX Designer

Chapter 7 · Resources
A collection of links and books for further study

We don't expect anyone to explore or learn everything presented in this book all at once. Learning UX Design is a journey where knowledge is accrued over time and experience. This book serves as a map of that journey so you can benefit from knowing what is out there and in what direction it lies. This book also serves as a ramp by helping you understand UX Design deeply and in a systematic way so you can learn and grow regardless if you are learning on your own, participating in workshops, or getting a formal education in UX Design or a related field.

Use the knowledge held in these pages to inspire you and kickstart your journey to become a UX Designer and reference it along the way to continue your growth. As part of your journey we would also love to hear your comments and suggestions for this book. If you have have any feedback, feel free to contact us at **chadandyujia@gmail.com**.

Thanks, and we hope you find great success!

– Chad and Yujia

1
Overview

"It's not enough that we build products that function, that are understandable and usable, we also need to build products that bring joy and excitement, pleasure and fun, and yes, beauty to people's lives."

Don Norman

What is UX Design?

UX, short for user experience, is a relatively new field that has been formed and developed along with the digital technology industry. In the digital product world, the "user experience" refers to how the product presents itself, how it works, and how people interact with it. The main goals of a good user experience are to provide some combination of efficiency, empowerment, enrichment, and enjoyment to the people who use the product. In other words, good user experience design can help people do things better, faster, more efficiently and effectively, or to do new things that cannot be done otherwise, all while enjoying the experience of learning and using the digital products and services.

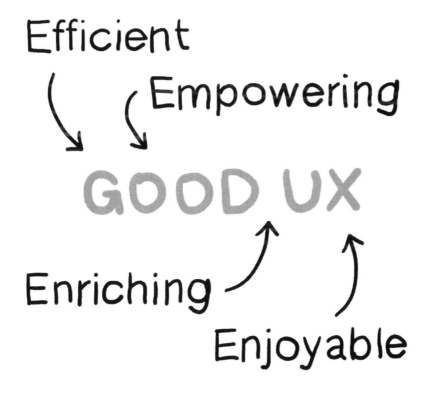

You will find that "UX Design" is defined by many different names, titles, and descriptions. Sometimes UX Design is defined as Interaction Design or User Interface Design but in truth those are design specializations within the field of UX Design. UX Design even at its simplest often includes user research, information architecture, UI design, interaction design, visual design, usability, accessibility, and copywriting. Taken even further UX Design is also concerned with how a product is marketed, sold, and taught. In our own experience we have even helped create strategies for customer service and support teams, since those teams also directly affect the user's experience.

UX Design is about addressing large and small problems with digital technology, but the anchor of UX Design is people. Your designs exist to serve people, and not just the primary users but also any other people it might direct or indirectly affect. This has given rise to the "user-centered" and broader "human-centered" design philosophies that encourage design approaches driven by the needs, wants, behaviors, and context of the people who make up the intended audience. This human-centered design philosophy is adopted and accepted pretty much by all UX Design practitioners, even if their actual practice and methods might differ.

Since the discipline of UX Design is still evolving, different companies or organizations sometimes put UX Design in different departments. However, regardless of how UX is treated or viewed at these companies, UX Design is one of the three pillars of digital product development together with product management and engineering. While product management handles the business aspect and engineering handles the implementation, UX teams handle the design of how the product works, looks, and feels. In effective, mature product organizations the three parties work closely together so that the product falls in the sweet spot of having a good user experience while providing business value and meeting technical constraints.

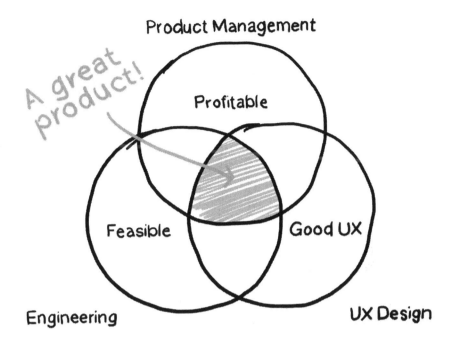

Product Management

A great product!

Profitable

Feasible

Good UX

Engineering

UX Design

What is a UX Designer?

If you are interested in UX Design, it is likely you have already come across many different definitions and terms to define what a UX Designer is and what they do. In fact, to a large degree all the definitions are accurate because UX is a discipline with a wide range of required job contributions and necessary skills. To make things simpler we just define UX Designer as the job function responsible for making UX Design decisions.

We consider UX Design to be an umbrella job function, and jobs like UI Design, Visual Design, UX Research, Usability Engineering, Prototyping, and Content Strategy to be specialized sub-job functions of UX Design. Typically the UX Designer doesn't do every single aspect of UX Design alone.

A UX Designer is aided by UX Researchers, who are responsible for conducting user studies and gathering data to inform the design. There are Visual and Graphic Designers, who are responsible for the graphic components of the product. There are UX Prototypers who are responsible for creating prototypes for testing and development purposes. There are Content Strategists and Copy Writers who are responsible for the language, words, tone, and translation of the user interface and other written collateral for the product.

In some jobs (typically more senior UX Design roles), the designer functions in a role similar to an architect. In these job roles the UX Designer is responsible for designing how the product works while being the hub of all other design job functions. Architects don't build the structures they design. They provide construction teams with blueprints to work from, much the same way that UX Designers provide design specifications to development teams.

Architects will design the interior layout of their buildings, but may leave carpet or curtain decisions to interior decorators. This is similar to how a UX Designer might provide wireframes for every screen of an application, but will rely on a visual designer to add the final visual style and graphic assets. And just like an architect, a senior UX Designer may be responsible for stewarding the design through the product development process to ensure the intended outcome.

However, there are many places, especially smaller companies and startups, where the UX Designer fulfills many of those specialized job functions themselves. Even at large organizations UX Designers may fill one or more of those specialized roles depending on the project or the available resources. That means that just like architects, UX Designers must have a working knowledge in many different fields such as research, visual design, psychology, business, engineering, and marketing. This is discussed further in Chapter 5.

While it is important for UX Designers to be knowledgeable about a wide variety of topics, you don't have to become good at everything. It is usually enough for UX Designers to become highly fluent in a few areas while maintaining working knowledge of the other areas.

There are many titles used in the industry for "UX Designer". A UX Designer may be referred to as UI Designer, Interaction Designer, Product Designer, Experience Designer, or even User Interface Engineer. Furthermore, you can't really read too much into the title as it won't necessarily reflect what exactly a person in that job at that company does. For instance you may find a "UI Design" job that consists of mainly research and marketing work, and an "Experience Design" job role that is actually a graphic design position.

Furthermore, some people with the title "UX Designer" do mostly production work and have no influence in the overall product direction, but there are others who wield greater influence than the Product Manager. It all depends on the organization and its needs, as well as the seniority of the designer.

While that may seem confusing, the good news is that a lot of the inconsistencies in our field should be temporary. As design teams and companies mature in their UX processes, job functions and titles will trend towards more standardized definitions. Because of this, for the purposes of this book we refer to UX Design as the field itself, and UX Designer as the person making UX Design decisions for digital products. There are also research, prototyping, graphic design, and UI-focused roles within the field, but we won't dissect the sub-job functions unless that particular topic lends itself to such a distinction.

Unique Challenges of UX Design

UX Designers enjoy very unique challenges. What follows is a short list of the challenges that UX Designers see every day, and knowing them ahead of time will help prepare you to become a UX Designer.

Ambiguity

"Design is an unknown."

- Geoffrey Beene

"You can't connect the dots looking forward; you can only connect them looking backwards. So you have to trust that the dots will somehow connect in your future."

- Steve Jobs

When you design you imagine and communicate something that currently doesn't exist. The creation process can be unpredictable, messy, and ambiguous up until the last moment. UX Designers must learn to embrace the beauty of ambiguity. To come up with something new the process of creation has to be unclear, at least for a little while. You must learn to trust that your process, methods, experience, and judgement will eventually help you find your way out of the woods. The resolution of ambiguities is one of the most rewarding parts of UX Design. It is a great feeling when you have that "Ah-ha!" moment when everything comes together and falls into place.

While ambiguity may be exhilarating to designers, the people designers work with don't always share the same feeling. People in other job functions handle ambiguity differently. Some will even actively avoid it. Some people like to know clearly what they are supposed to do and how they are supposed to do it. This is often true of companies who want safe, predictable paths to success and profit, and for software teams who deal with the specifics of code.

For example, we have been in situations where a key decision maker wanted to see designs but we only had rough sketches. When we showed them he wasn't happy because he couldn't see where the design was going. He wanted to know exactly what it would look like, and furthermore to know the reasoning behind every single decision.

You could say that he "had no imagination", but the fact was he wasn't comfortable moving forward without seeing the full high-fidelity details, with research that "proved" that the design was the right thing to do. Now of course, in situations like this part of the problem was that it was just too early to show the design. However, in the end design can't happen without making decisions. It is not only the UX Designer's job to make design decisions with ambiguity, but to make other stakeholders comfortable with those decisions.

Real vs. Ideal

Design happens in the real world. Here are some common aspects of the "real world" that are often seen with UX Design problems:

People are complicated.

"Design is directed toward human beings. To design is to solve human problems by identifying them and executing the best solution."

- Ivan Chermayeff

Your designs serve people's needs, and those needs are complex. It is of little use to go out and ask them, "What do you need?" What they say might not be what they mean, and one person's view can be very different from another's. This is why it is important to be fluent in the various user research methods outlined in Chapter 4.

Each problem is unique.

You are always designing for a particular problem or domain space, each with its own complexities and nuances. Each new project requires research and understanding of the unique needs of the situation. This is one of the many challenges that makes UX Design so rewarding. Each new problem you work on exposes you to more of the world.

But you must be patient and diligent. If you are designing in a domain you are unfamiliar with, it may take a while to become knowledgeable enough to design effective solutions. For a grand example, if you need to design something related to the American healthcare system it could take months to get a grasp of the basics. (But that expertise would make you a highly-valued designer!)

You don't work in a vacuum.

Designers work within the existing team dynamic and environment. In addition to your target users, there are product managers, programmers, fellow designers, researchers, marketers, and high-level management that all have an interest in shaping the product. While it is exciting and rewarding to collaborate with so many people, it can also be a complicated task to design solutions as a team with internal and external stakeholders. Any given project is likely to face changes in project scope and requirements.

Designers must learn how to deal with all the stakeholders' feedback. What do you do when you get feedback you don't agree with? What if that if that feedback comes from a VIP stakeholder, like the CEO?

You work within constraints.

"Here is one of the few effective keys to the design problem: the ability of the designer to recognize as many of the constraints as possible; his willingness and enthusiasm for working within these constraints."

- Charles Eames

Good designers know that design can't happen without constraints. Constraints are the guide rails around the problem space designers work within, and good designers embrace them even if they seem unfair or unreasonable. You may have to design for legacy systems that can't provide the speed or flexibility you would like to have. You may have to adjust the language to adhere to marketing and branding guidelines. You might not be able to use a particular interaction because it is patented, or you may be forced to add extra screens to your UI to deal with license agreements and legal information.

Truth be told, it isn't the difficult constraints that cause problems for UX Designers. The real tricky constraints are the ones that are not clearly defined, or are given but actually are negotiable. For example, you might be told that your design solution must not require changes to the database because it is too costly. You could very well design to that constraint, provide a good solution, and make everyone happy. However, if you were to consider that constraint to be negotiable you might come up with a better solution that increases profits enough to offset the cost of the changes to the database. Good designers always think about the "what ifs" with regards to constraints, know which ones are negotiable, and seek out missing constraints.

You must combine the subjective and objective.

While there are some fields that emphasize either objectivity (math, physics) or subjectivity (art, anthropology), UX Design is a field that pulls from both. UX Designers need to balance the two and know when they should be applied during research and design. For example, objectively a usability test can tell you that "12 out of 15 users couldn't find the button," but you may also need to gather subjective data from interviews or surveys to discover why this occurred.

UX Designers and Researchers utilize design research that deals with subjective matters such as emotions and motivations, but it likely needs to be quantified in some manner to be useful in making design decisions. For instance, if you interview 10 people and ask what motivates them to sign into their email every day you will get a lot of different subjective answers. However, you might categorize their answers into summary data, so you can make an objective statement such as, "7 out of 10 users reported they are motivated to check their email daily hoping to hear from family or friends."

As in the previous example, in order to make sense of large amounts of data it usually has to be quantified even if the research questions deal with subjective matters. However, regardless of how the data is quantified the interpretation of data is subjective. It is up to the UX Designer's judgment and experience to see into the research findings and find inspiration for solutions.

2
Learning
Advice

"I am always doing that which I can not do, in order that I may learn how to do it."

Pablo Picasso

UX Design is a practical yet very thoughtful discipline, and a UX Designer's single most important skill is the ability to learn and adapt. The best advice we can give for learning UX Design is to absorb design information, practice design methods and techniques, and reflect upon your practice. The following section offers details and advice for those three activities based on our own experiences, interviews with fellow UX professionals, and our own interests in effective learning techniques.

As you learn and grow as a designer, remember that learning UX Design is a journey. It takes time, patience, and experience to grow into a fully competent UX Designer. This chapter provides advice to speed up your learning process and make your journey smooth and enjoyable.

Absorb

A lot of UX learning happens through "absorption", which is to acquire information through reading, listening, or watching. This is probably the easiest activity of the three because UX Design is an open community with an abundance of learning material. Since there is more info available than anyone could possibly absorb, you should focus on what you need to improve upon as well as what inspires you.

To get you started we have provided a list of our recommended UX Design books in Chapter 7 as well as other reference material. Feel free to follow any design blogs you find inspirational to stay up to date on design.

Reading is a necessity, but it isn't enough just to read everything about UX Design. Make it a point to attend some workshops, conferences, and talks related to UX Design. They aren't hard to find. Believe us, there is always somebody looking for an audience to listen to them talk about design! (Look at us, we felt the need to write a book about it.) If you are currently working and your company has a UX team, observe the UX Designers there and ask them questions about how they do their work.

While absorbing the information out there, don't be discouraged when you find discrepancies between sources. For example, information about how to conduct a card sorting research session might be described differently between this book and another book or website. This is common and normal, as many methods are borrowed and adapted from other fields such as anthropology and sociology for the needs of UX Design, and they constantly evolve and change through practice over time. UX Design is not and never will be an exact science.

Practice

> "The attained level of performance of many types of experts - is closely related to their accumulated amount of deliberate practice."
>
> - K.A. Ericsson

You have to practice to get better at design. This is the most crucial activity among the three. Without practice, it doesn't matter how much you read and how much you think. Even if you currently are not in the industry or you are not in school for UX Design, there are still many ways you can practice.

Work on a personal project.
Is there an application that you use that you really want to improve? Try redesigning it. Is there a group of people you want to help or serve through digital products? Go interview them to find out their needs and design a solution for them. Do you have an app idea or a website you want to make? Make some sketches, prototype it, and test it.

There is absolutely nothing stopping you from designing new solutions for any of those situations. If you are concerned about not being good enough yet, understand that is the reason why you practice. Personal projects don't need to have any pressure (other than the pressure you put on yourself). You don't even need to show it to anybody if you don't want to, although we do encourage you to show it to the intended audience to get feedback. What is important is that you gain experience through intentional practice.

Design something for family or friends.

If you don't have a personal project you want to work on, you can ask people you know if they need some design help. It is likely that you know someone who has a website or mobile app in need of a redesign. Maybe you know someone with a business that doesn't have a site or app at all. Offer to design it for them.

Participate in design competitions.

There are many student and professional design competitions hosted by design websites, companies, and schools that provide a great opportunity to practice design with real world problems (as well as the chance to win money, and sometimes free travel). Even if you don't win you still get the benefit of practice as well as a portfolio piece. Also, you can learn a lot from studying the winning design as well as all the other entries.

Even in real jobs, there are rarely any projects that start with just an idea, go through the full design process, and end with full visuals or working UIs. This means that you don't need to attempt to practice every method or the whole process during a given project. Even if you only design a simple form on a web page, it is still worth doing and you will learn something.

UX Design practice has a cumulative learning effect. If you learned how to do usability testing in one project, and designed form field validation in another, over time all of those small exercises will add up to well-rounded practical knowledge and experience.

Another thing worth mentioning is that absorbing and practice should go hand in hand to get better results. If you just finished reading about the card sorting method, we encourage you to practice it right away. If you are designing a contact form for a project, you should look for articles on form design to guide and inspire you. Simultaneously absorbing and practicing will help you really master the knowledge and skills as your own because you learned it not only through reading or practicing, but from both.

Reflect

"The idea of reflection—suggests a direction of inquiry into processes which tend otherwise to be mystified and dismissed with the terms intuition or creativity."

- Donald Schön

"We do not learn from experience, we learn from reflecting on experience."

- John Dewey

Conventional wisdom says that if you practice something enough you will get better, but this is not entirely true. Only practice combined with reflection upon that practice leads to improvement. Practice without reflection is merely repetition, which is a guaranteed way to develop bad habits. However, if you ask yourself how you did and where you could improve, you will be prepared the next time to do it better or at least to try something different to see if you get a better result.

Reflection is relatively easy. After you practice you should ask yourself questions like: What skills and knowledge did I apply? What worked well and what didn't? How well did I collaborate with others? Were there any areas I want to improve in? A great technique for this is to write your reflections in a diary or blog. When you sit down and formulate your thoughts in writing, it helps you think deeply and gives you a place to preserve your thoughts. It is rewarding to look back months or years later on where you were and see how much you have grown.

In the words of researcher and philosopher Donald Schön, this is called "reflection-on-action". Reflection-on-action is basically "reflecting on the actions you have taken at some point in the past". His quote at the beginning of this section refers to how, as designers, reflection helps us to demystify how we create things and solve problems. In demystifying the design process we can more easily repeat our successes, build upon our abilities, and confidently make decisions.

There is a second type of reflection that is just as critical as the first, and Schön called this "reflection-in-action". Reflection-in-action is basically "reflecting on actions in the moment" or "thinking on your feet". Reflection-in-action is all about situational awareness, or in other words being mindful about what is currently happening. You don't have to wait until something is over to reflect upon it. While you are practicing design, reading, or having a conversation it is natural to have some out-of-the-moment thoughts about the current situation.

Everyone does this, but most people tend to ignore the feelings as passing thoughts or a lack of focus. Reflection-in-action is not "being distracted", but instead is a deliberate recognition of when those thoughts should be focused on, at least for a moment, to gain some insight about the situation.

For example, imagine you are conducting a user interview. If you have trained your situational awareness and are paying attention, you might notice that the participant seems to be a little tense. Because you noticed this, in the moment you might ask yourself why and find that you can do something to alleviate the tension. You might offer a light smile or offer the participant something to drink.

Or perhaps the questions you are asking are somehow contributing to the participant's tension. Someone who doesn't reflect-in-action might not notice and will just "stick to the script", perhaps leading to poor answers or even upsetting the participant. Someone who does reflect-in-action might recognize that the question script is not viable for this interview session, and instead could improvise new questions on the spot.

For another example, imagine you are designing a particular screen and feel pretty good about the interaction you designed. You might pause for a moment to think about why you think it is so good. Maybe you feel a keen sense of the problem it addresses, and you can clearly see the positive impact it had and how it solved the problem so well. Because you reflected in that moment about the design, at that point you might add it to your library of design solutions so you could apply what you learned in the moment at a later time.

Situational reflection is also very useful for facilitating team collaboration. It is common for people to get caught up in the moment during meetings, and conversations may run long and off-topic. Sometimes the conversation can stall and frustrate people, but they may not even know it is happening. Good designers (and professionals in all fields) are situationally aware enough to take a pause, step back, and think about what is happening.

Internally and even externally to the group, they ask questions like: Is everyone on the same page about what is important? Do we know what we are trying to decide here? Is someone disagreeing because of some unspoken concerns? Should we take a break and come back to this topic? Your conscious reflection in the moment will not only help improve the current situation, but also help you improve your analytical, collaboration, facilitation, and leadership skills.

These two types of reflection together are necessary catalysts for growing and learning not only your design skills, but in general your overall abilities and competency. Make reflection part of your regular habits, but remember you don't have to do it all by yourself. If you have a blog you can invite others to read and share their thoughts. You can get coffee with some designer friends to talk about your work and what you currently think about design.

And by all means, don't limit your conversations just to fellow designers. Talk to your non-design friends, parents, or relatives. We have had small and large epiphanies on design while explaining what we do to parents, doctors, and even strangers in the airport.

The right attitude

Most of the advice here applies to other fields of learning as well, but they are particularly important for learning UX Design. Learning design is not a matter of memorizing facts or processes. Design isn't like math or science where there are processes and paths to arrive at a "correct" answer. UX Design involves understanding problems and creating solutions that address them, but there will never be a "correct" answer to a design challenge. To practice and learn design, you have to adopt a certain attitude towards learning.

Be Patient

The learning methods described in this chapter are by no means revolutionary. However, perseverance is also needed due to the amount of time and persistence it takes to see progress, especially when that progress is not linear. One month of work may not feel like a month of progress. Instead, you will experience breakthroughs and plateaus. At first it may be hard to judge how you are getting better but you must keep at it. After you build up some experience you will look back on your work and see how far you have come.

> "Nobody tells this to people who are beginners...All of us who do creative work, we get into it because we have good taste. But there is this gap. For the first couple years you make stuff, it's just not that good. It's trying to be good, it has potential, but it's not. But your taste, the thing that got you into the game, is still killer. And your taste is why your work disappoints you. A lot of people never get past this phase, they quit. Most people I know who do interesting, creative work went through years of this. We know our work doesn't have this special thing that we want it to have. We all go through this. And if you are just starting out or you are still in this phase, you gotta know it's normal and **the most important thing you can do is do a lot of work**."
>
> - Ira Glass

Be Balanced

It is imperative to find balance between your UX knowledge, skills, and tools. If you have been learning tools for a while, make sure to think about what knowledge you should catch up on. Alternately, if you have been reading, talking, and thinking about design a lot maybe it is time to get your hands dirty making a prototype using a new tool.

Be Open

Every discipline has its own rigor, which is its own systematic approach and set ways of doing things. This rigor is manifested in the principles, best practices, methods, and theories of the field. Each field's training and experience help establish a set of attitude and philosophy in one, which is called "mindset".

Everyone learning UX Design has some kind of training or education in other disciplines, meaning you already have a mindset and notion of rigor that will affect how you perceive the field of UX Design. Since the mindset of UX Design is a unique, sometimes even conflicting blend of art, history, psychology, sociology, and empirical observation it is important not to rigidly apply your already-learned knowledge, methodologies, or mental models to UX Design. Methods and philosophies that are held to be true in one discipline don't necessarily work for another.

Always keep an open mind and be aware of the unique mindset and rigor of UX Design. If you encounter something that you perceive to be illogical (or even stupid), try to withhold judgement until you really understand why it is that way.

Be Humble

To be a UX Designer you must be able to let go of ideas and see things from others' point of view. Ego can be a large hurdle for many designers. Everyone has an ego, be it large or small, and since UX Designers pour bits of themselves into their work it is easy for ego to develop. It is easy to grow attached to your own ideas and follow your own logic about the way things should be. Nobody likes being wrong. But UX Designers must not only accept being wrong, they must embrace it.

Ego can be a very dangerous thing when learning UX Design. Ego can stop you from reflecting on your own mistakes or learning from others. Ego can prevent you from providing the best solution because it will tell you that you don't really need to listen to what users say with their words or actions. Ego can make others wary of collaborating with you because it will prevent you from listening and respecting others. Always remember to be humble and let go of your ego. The moment you let your ego get the best of you is the moment you stop growing.

3
The Design
Process

"Designers don't actually solve problems. They work through them."

Marty Neumeier

The purpose of this chapter is to provide an in-depth explanation of how the design process happens. We use the term "process" here, but we want to emphasize that although the term process often implies something that is repeatable and linear, the design process is not exactly either of those. This is one of the many reasons that UX Designers must be comfortable with ambiguity and flexible in their design approach.

To discuss the design process, we feel it is important to begin with four principles that apply to any UX Design process, no matter where it takes place:

1. The design process varies by project.

The specific steps in a process that works for one project might not work for another. If you are designing an online whiteboard tool for remote collaboration, you might want to start the design process with contextual inquiry, participating in remote meetings with your target users to see what things are like in context. But if you are designing a shopping cart checkout experience, there is likely no need for contextual inquiry. You might start with a prototype and use that to test and gather feedback.

2. A strict design process rarely works.

A strict design process assumes that the problems to be solved are static or similar, and that the designer or product team's skill set is fairly predictable. This is not the norm. Digital product development teams often have rapidly changing requirements, staffing, and resources.

In addition, designers have different experience, knowledge, and philosophies on design. A UX Designer with a lot of design experience in the eCommerce field will spend less time researching existing shopping cart examples than someone who has never designed in the field at all. Even two designers with similar backgrounds might still choose to do things differently. One might choose to do paper sketches to gather feedback before committing to a high-fidelity rendering, and the other might choose to start with a prototype made with HTML/CSS and make changes based on that. A strict design process would prevent designers (and product teams) from working in the most effective manner to make use of their own unique skillsets.

3. The design process is not linear.

It is very common to go back and forth between activities. Designers move between research, testing, ideation, and production phases as needed in order to create a solid solution. For example you might be at the wireframing stage and realize some key information was missing, requiring you to conduct more research. Or you might be in the testing phase and come up with a much better design solution, requiring you to explore new concepts before pushing the current design forward.

4. The design process happens in the real world.

UX Design is intertwined with the product development process in the real world. Some designers make the mistake of trying to establish the "ideal" design process with product teams, requiring robust phases of research, concept generation, and testing. As pure as the motives are, what usually happens when these designers push for the ideal is that their ideal requires "enough" research, or "enough" concepts, or "enough" testing to make decisions.

In truth, the best design process is one that uses the available time and resources as effectively as possible to achieve a quality result. For example, on some projects you might not get to be involved from the very beginning to the very end. Sometimes you join a project towards the end, and your job is to refine the UI detail and produce final specs. You can't explore other concepts at the expense of delivering within the timeline.

The Double Diamond Model

Even though the design process may be unpredictable and non-linear, there are commonalities between all design processes. To describe the design process we expand upon the widely understood and adopted Double Diamond Model put together by the UK Design Council. This is an overall framework and structure that is commonly seen in most design practices and is proven to produce good results.

There are countless other design process models out there, but we chose to build upon this model because it best reflects the nature of the design process in that it is descriptive, not prescriptive. It is general enough to apply to most if not all manner of design projects, large or small, with only slight modifications. Most companies, organizations, and design agencies follow a design process similar to the Double Diamond Model even if they don't know it by name or are fluent in every phase.

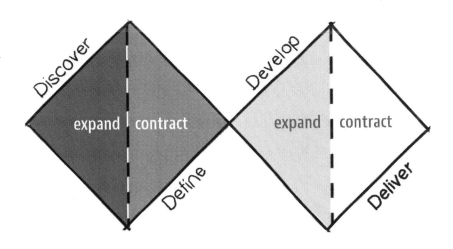

As you can see, the design process is made up of 4 phases–Discover, Define, Develop, and Deliver. The Discover and Develop phases involve activities that expand possibilities, while the Define and Deliver phases reduce them. While there is some linearity to the model, depending on the situation or project there is typically movement back and forth between phases.

There is seldom a design project that treats each phase with equal weight. The actual process could take on many forms depending on the needs of the project or on the structure of the product development process. For example, there may be a relatively small research phase with a very large concept phase. Or the process may start with a really great concept that just needs some definition and then heads straight into the Deliver phase. When working with Agile development teams you often repeat the Develop and Deliver phases as the product is built in pieces.

EXAMPLE VARIATIONS OF THE DOUBLE DIAMOND MODEL IN THE REAL WORLD

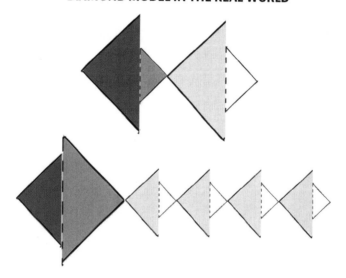

Regardless of how exactly it plays out, each phase has particular goals, methods, principles, and activities. There isn't always a clear distinction between the phases, but it is important for UX Designers to be able to recognize what phase the project is currently in, where it should be, and what decisions need to be made in order to move forward.

The rest of this chapter explains the purpose and activities of each phase. There may be methods and activities mentioned here that you are not familiar with. They are expanded upon in Chapter 4.

The Discover Phase

"He who asks a question is a fool for five minutes; he who does not ask a question remains a fool forever."

- Chinese Proverb

The purpose of this phase is to ask questions, acquire information, and form a basic understanding of the project and the problem to be addressed. The Discover Phase is the foundation of the following phases. The primary outcome of this phase is a good understanding of the problem space. With the information you collect you will be able to plan your process with the appropriate activities to help you define the problem, describe users and core scenarios, and distill design insights that are crucial for orienting you towards a good design solution.

During the Discover Phase, pretty much all design projects need to uncover the following information:

- The design problem to be solved
- Business value and requirements
- Project timeline, resources, and constraints
- Users and their context

The Design Problem to be Solved

What is the problem you need to address? This is the vital question, and without an answer your design will have no direction or target. Knowing the problem gets you half of the way towards solving it. A clear definition of the design problem can be just as elusive as its solution, and the design problem statement at the end of the Discover Phase is rarely the same problem statement from the beginning.

Business Value and Requirements

The business needs and goals directly and indirectly influence the design. Understanding the business context will help you see how your design supports the goals of the business, and will make your collaboration with product managers easier. What is the value of this product or service? What problem will it solve for the customers or users? How will success be measured?

Project Timeline, Resources, and Constraints

The design solution is affected by how much time you are allowed, what resources (people and materials) you have access to, as well as many other constraints. For example, if the project has a lengthy timeline you might get to do three rounds of usability testing with multiple users. However in short timelines you might be lucky just to get feedback from a single user by showing a sketch to a stranger in a coffee shop. As a designer sometimes you just take what you can get.

Some of these constraints are likely to change as the project proceeds, and you will likely need to adjust your approach accordingly. While design can't happen without constraints, keep in mind that you don't always have to bend to whatever constraints are imposed upon you. It is important to identify problematic constraints during the Discover Phase. Many constraints are negotiable, and it is the UX Designer's responsibility to speak up and justify why they might negatively affect the design outcome.

Users and Their Context

Your design serves the users in their context, so it is important to have an understanding about them. You will investigate and understand their needs, goals, and even their fears. You will need to understand as much about their context as possible, such as what other tools they use in the context, how comfortable they are with computers, or how they work with other people.

Activities During This Phase

If you work in a corporate environment it is likely that the business requirements, timeline, resources, and constraints will be provided from the cross-functional team, most commonly the product manager. In an agency environment you typically get that information from your client.

If there is not enough information internally about the design problem and the user, you and your team will probably conduct your own research to discover this information. It is typically up to the UX Design or Research team to come up with a study or research plan outlining what information needs to be uncovered, what questions to ask, what methods to use, and how to recruit participants.

There are various research methods and techniques you can choose from depending on the particular project you work on. Chapter 4 discusses research methods and techniques in more detail, but some common ones to know are interviews, contextual inquiry, and surveys.

Designers also frequently need to design their own research activities to get the type of data they need. For example, the following image shows a "product map" research activity we came up to understand how we could unify workflows between multiple disparate products. In this activity we provided users with a magnetic activity board to semantically describe and organize the products they use in their everyday workflows.

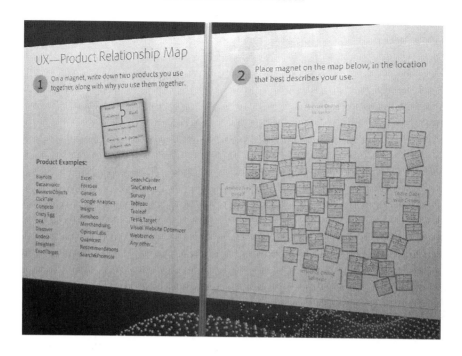

When you get information directly from users it is referred to as primary research, but you can also do secondary research. This is when you look at other people's research findings or existing information. For example, you might be designing a website that sells cars but you aren't fluent in all the various car types. All it takes is a quick Internet search on "car types" to save you lots of time rather than relying on your client or the product manager to explain it to you. Another type of secondary research could be to do competitive analysis of other car sales websites.

Product managers and UX Researchers are key collaborators in this phase. Sometimes you might not be the one leading the research effort, but UX Designers should participate in as much research as possible. Reading a report from the researcher is not nearly as valuable as discovering the information first-hand.

Tips for the Discover Phase

- Identify what you don't know.
- Learn to listen.
- Don't dwell on ideas.
- Be creative about how to collect information.

Identify what you don't know.

You should think deeply about the problem to identify what you already know, and more importantly what you don't know. Plan your research to get information on what you don't know and to validate what you think you already know.

Conducting research and gleaning information from users is an art form. You rarely get the information you need by asking users directly about the problem, and different research methods can give you different kinds of data. For instance survey data can tell you surface level information about a group of people, while interviews are better for understanding why someone does something on a deeper level.

Learn to listen.

Listen with an open mind. During the Discover Phase don't let your preconceived notions prevent you from really hearing what the users, product manager, and team members are saying.

Don't dwell on ideas.

UX Designers tend to be solution-focused people. It is natural to come up with ideas about how the problem can be solved during the Discover Phase. Make note of them, but don't dwell on them or get attached to any one idea. The main goal of the Discover Phase is to collect information, discover, and understand the problem.

Be creative about how to collect information.

Every design project is unique, and often the best research methods will also be unique. If you can't get the information you need using the existing research methods, come up with your own methods.

If you need to understand the user's pain points, maybe you host a session where users place Post-it notes with their pain points on a special chart you designed. Maybe it would be beneficial to observe users going through some tasks with competitors' products instead of your own. You can even show the users a prototype of some early ideas you have if you think that will help you discover information more effectively.

The Define Phase

{ "The greatest challenge to any thinker is stating the problem in a way that will allow a solution."

- Bertrand Russell }

After the Discover Phase you will have at least a basic understanding of the problem, context, and users along with lots of data at your disposal. But data alone is worthless. Data must be synthesized into information, and information must be turned into actionable insights. That is the goal of the Define Phase, where the outcome is typically some kind of design brief that clearly articulates the problem and how the team plans to address the problem (both at a high level and detailed level as appropriate).

The design brief should be a mutually agreed-upon document that the team can refer to throughout the project to ensure everyone stays on the proper path. However, it can and should be altered, changed, and revised as the project progresses and the team learns more. There is no formal template for design briefs, but it is a document that typically includes the following information:

- Problem statement
- Descriptions of your target users
- Your target users' goals and key workflows
- The user pain points that will be addressed by the design
- The main design constraints you must work within
- The main design goals
- Design principles to follow

Activities During This Phase

There are many research and design methods to help you clean up, organize, and analyze data in order to distill insights. For example, if you have lots of disparate, scattered data points you can consider using Affinity Diagrams to organize them. Affinity Diagrams are a way of grouping lots of small data points to give a structured view of the data you collected, making it easier to discover insights.

You are very likely to produce personas based on the data you collected about the users. (You can also do this as part of Discover Phase.) Just like most UX Design methods, there is no "one size fits all" approach to creating personas. We have used dozens of different persona types, and the way you construct a persona depends largely on the needs of the project and the design problem.

For example, if you are designing a survey tool for a "Marketing Researcher" persona it might be useful to include the other tools they use in their everyday work so you can better integrate those tools with your product. In this example, if your Marketing Researcher persona uses Microsoft Excel for data analysis, you may see that importing Excel .*csv* files into your tool will be valuable to your user.

However, if you are designing an eCommerce site for young people who are into Gothic fashion, it isn't crucial to include the different software tools they use. Instead, it might be more important to include descriptions of their lifestyle or purchasing habits.

If your users' workflows are complex and varied, you can consider using Storyboards and Flow Diagrams to visualize them. When you have the whole journey mapped out in front of you on paper or a whiteboard, it will be easier to see what areas are problematic and how can you improve their flow with your design solutions.

You should document your key findings as you go since you will likely refer back to them when you work on solutions in the Develop and Deliver Phases. As mentioned earlier, it is beneficial to write a design brief that includes a statement of the problem you are solving, key personas, scenarios, insights, and design principles. The design brief should be kept short (one page at maximum), which forces you to be concise and focus on the key elements of the design. It is much easier to reference later when it is short.

You should read the design brief often, ideally before any design activities or meetings. The design brief is not meant to be absolute. As the product team's understanding changes and grows, so too should the design brief.

Tips for the Define Phase

- Data must be interpreted to be of any use.
- Work with others.
- There is no such thing as "the right amount" of data.
- Assumptions are OK.

Data must be interpreted to be of any use.

The Discover Phase generates a lot of data, but without your interpretation the insights will not reveal themselves. Try to balance objective data and subjective interpretation.

Work with others.

Other people's interpretation might be different from yours. Discuss your findings with others and try to understand other people's thought processes. Cross-pollination of thoughts always reveals deeper insights.

There is no such thing as "the right amount" of data.

You will never have enough data to feel 100 percent confident about every decision you need to make. As previously mentioned, UX Designers must make decisions and move forward knowing that there is some level of ambiguity. You can go back to research and data collection if you feel you don't have the insights you need, but don't fool yourself into thinking that the insights will emerge by themselves when you have "enough" data.

Assumptions are OK.

We will continue to iterate that UX Designers have to make decisions, and those decisions often are based on (informed) assumptions. You don't have to, and are unable to back up every single decision with data. This is where your team's and your judgment and trust of each other is important.

There are no standards or rules around which assumptions are OK to make and what which are not. It is important to voice and discuss them with your team. If you and your team feel confident about them, put them in the design brief and move forward. If you change those assumptions later on, then change the design brief accordingly.

The Develop Phase

{ "No idea is so outlandish that it should not be considered with a searching but at the same time steady eye."

- Winston Churchill }

By the end of Define Phase you should have a quality design brief outlining the problem, users, key scenarios, and design goals. You likely even have many design ideas you jotted down along the way. Now is the time where you use all that input to fuel your creativity and problem solving in the Develop and Deliver Phases. This is many designer's favorite phase because this is when the designer puts their production and creativity skills to work sketching, mocking up, and prototyping design solutions.

To be clear, the word "Develop" in this design process model refers to "maturing", or "growing" a design concept. We don't intend to conflate this with the software industry connotation of develop to mean "programming or producing software code". While UX Design and Software Development are intertwined, developing or maturing a design concept is different than developing code. (Although you may decide to use code to explore a design concept.)

The purpose of the Develop Phase is to work through many design directions and solutions, making decisions as you look for the best design. The outcome of the Develop Phase is a singular, validated design direction (the best design). By "best design" we don't mean the absolute best, most perfect design. You may have heard the famous quote from Voltaire that, "Perfect is the enemy of good." Well in software development perfect is also the enemy of "done", which more often than not is more important than "good."

In truth, the best way to think about the best or good design is to arrive at a design that "satisfices", which simply means the design is good enough to practically and sufficiently satisfy the needs of the problem as it is defined. The definition of what qualifies as satisficing is left up to the UX Designer and the rest of the product team.

UX Designers help the product team arrive at this singular design direction by exploring lots of solutions and narrowing them down through iteration and evaluation. It is imperative to explore multiple concepts during the Develop Phase, because there are essentially infinite was to solve any particular problem. Out of those infinite solutions the vast majority are bad, some are good, and a tiny few of them are truly genius. With so many bad solutions available it is difficult to arrive at a good one on your first try, and virtually impossible to come up with a genius one. Even if you get lucky on one project, you likely won't be lucky on the next.

Activities During This Phase

This phase is all about making decisions to maintain forward momentum. This is the time to explore, sketch, prototype, evaluate, eliminate, and iterate upon ideas.

Sketching & brainstorming

Sketching and brainstorming activities are the most effective ways to get lots of ideas in a short amount of time. When you sketch you typically don't worry about the quality of ideas, but instead just focus on quantity. The main goal is to generate lots of ideas, as many as possible and as different as possible.

Exemplar Study

Besides coming up with ideas on your own or with your team, you should also study similar and related designs out there for inspiration. It is common practice to refer to similar designs in the same domain (competitive analysis), but there are designs in unrelated domains that might be inspirational in their own way.

For example, in our careers we have designed several information dashboards. While we certainly looked at dashboards from within the domain (marketing, web analytics, or IT administration), we also found inspiration in unrelated domains like websites used by surfers to identify tide and wave patterns. Seeing how problems are solved in other domains can help spark new ideas and ways to solve problems in the domain you are designing for.

Prototyping

The reason you come up with lots of solutions is so you can select one or more to evolve. There are lots of prototyping methods and tools to choose from to do this. For the purposes of the Develop Phase, you should pick whatever prototyping method is the most efficient to produce, with enough fidelity necessary to convey the design concept.

You will quickly realize that you can't prototype all your ideas. Discard the ideas that aren't good enough. Some ideas may be equally good but very similar, so you might want to prototype just one or two from them. Idea A and Idea B may be very different concepts, but perhaps it is hard to say which one is better. You can prototype them both, test them, and find out.

Evaluation

During the Develop Phase you are only looking for feedback that helps you evaluate, eliminate, and iterate upon ideas. Depending on what kinds of products you are working on, during the Develop Phase there is seldom a need for robust or perfect testing plans. You don't need to test the details, because you are just trying to evaluate if the design is headed in the right direction.

You can get a lot of great feedback from users by just putting your prototypes in front of them and observing, listening, and following your instincts. As long as your evaluation methods aren't biased or flawed, you will get the feedback you need to keep moving.

There may be times when more formal testing is required, but during the Develop Phase UX Designers shouldn't become overly reliant upon them. Evaluation during the Develop Phase should be conducted in a manner that is fast and efficient.

Tips for the Develop Phase

- Dedicate enough time for brainstorming and exploration.
- Feedback and iteration should be fast and frequent.
- Focus on the core problem, scenarios, and how it works (leave the details for later).

Dedicate enough time for brainstorming and exploration.

If you spend very little time on exploration, you will likely end up implementing a poor solution. If a poor solution gets implemented in code then that leads to a lot of second-guessing that will drag down or doom the project. You might really like the first idea or two, but you must force yourself to come up with more. Get other stakeholders involved to cross-pollinate ideas.

Feedback and iteration should be fast and frequent.

You don't need to write up formal study plans with perfectly-designed test cases, and you don't need shiny, polished prototypes. Only prototype and test the minimum amount to get the feedback you need so you can iterate, make decisions, and move forward.

Focus on the core problem, scenarios, and how it works.

Far too often UX Designers (and other stakeholders) start to focus on visual design and edge cases during the Develop Phase before they have really solved the core problem or accounted for the core scenarios. To borrow a phrase from Bill Buxton, this is the difference between getting the "right design" versus getting the "design right".

The Develop Phase is not the time to perfect the alignment of the page header or to figure out how to deal with users who forget their password. The main purpose of this phase is to explore and then narrow down ideas and directions. If you get too hung up on details it will distract you from what is important, and you can't solve the overall problem if you are dealing with the minutiae of design details. Those details should be left until the Deliver Phase, when you fully polish your design.

The Deliver Phase

{ "The details are not the details. They make the design."

- Charles Eames }

By the end of the Develop Phase you should feel confident about the concept and the direction the design is heading. However, just having a low-fidelity prototype or a set of wireframes is not a full design solution yet. If the Develop Phase is about getting the "right" or "best" design direction, the Deliver Phase is about getting the "design right" by improving, refining, and polishing the rough design into the final design and communicating it in a comprehensive manner.

The outcome of the Deliver Phase is a thorough design solution covering all scenarios, with visual design included, clearly communicated in whatever format is most appropriate for your product team or audience of stakeholders.

In order to get from the design concept in the Develop Phase to the final design, the Deliver Phase is a journey of continuous iteration, decision making, and refinement. You will build upon the low-fidelity rendering and produce refined UI mockups or high-fidelity prototypes so that the final experience is represented.

Activities During This Phase

Testing
During the Deliver Phase you typically conduct usability testing on a high-fidelity prototype to help you discover any outstanding usability flaws. After a few rounds of testing and iteration, you will be able to solidify and polish the design.

Covering all the use cases
The Deliver Phase is when you fill in all the screens for secondary paths and scenarios, as well as edge cases, errors, system failure handling, and even legal requirements. The amount of detail required for these depends on the product team, but every detail counts.

Visual Design and Copy
At this stage visual design and copywriting should be finalized in addition to the UI interactions and layout. This is typically done when you feel there will not be any major interaction design-related changes. Visual design and copy should be tested as well by incorporating them into your high-fidelity prototype to see how users react to them. You will need to make sure you account for existing visual, branding, and copywriting guidelines in the design deliverables.

Stewarding the Design
Depending on the team structure and rank of the designer, the UX Designer may serve as a "steward" or "director" during the Deliver Phase. If you have a small team you may take on most of the roles on your own, but in many jobs visual design, copywriting, testing, and prototyping are handled by dedicated job functions. If this is the case you will collaborate with other roles, and it is imperative that as the UX Designer you protect the integrity of the design direction throughout the process.

Instead of throwing the design "over the wall" to visual designers, copywriters, and developers, the UX Designer should ensure that all parties involved understand the experiential quality of the design, who the target users are, and how it works so that all elements are consistent with the overall design. During this phase you will work with others and offer feedback, but should understand in some job situations the final approval may belong to another job function. That is one of the reasons why it is so imperative for UX Designers to be good facilitators and communicators.

If you work with a prototyper or user researcher, you will need to explain exactly how the design works and what parts of the UI are key for testing, and what parts could be "faked" to produce an appropriate prototype within the least amount of time.

Documentation & Specifications

Throughout the design process the UX Designer communicates the design in various ways at different stages for cross-team collaboration and research. However, during the Deliver Phase it is likely required that you comprehensively document and communicate how the design works. This documentation is used by software programming teams to know what to implement, by quality assurance teams to know what to test against, and by product management and other cross-functional teams to reference as needed for their job function.

This documentation can take many forms. The most common is a design specification document in which you use wireframes, mockups, flow diagrams, text descriptions, and other visuals to explain how the design works. Design specifications should be concise but accurate, and focus solely on how it works and how to build it.

The format you will use is largely dependent upon your time and skills, and what is appropriate for the project, the team, and the company. No matter what format you choose, you also should have effective ways to update and communicate changes. It is unlikely that you can cover every single detail, and there will be updates due to unforeseen technical constraints and product requirement changes.

If you work closely with a development team that uses Agile or Lean design approaches, you may find that you don't need to create a lot of specifications. Lean UX approaches seek to minimize the amount of documentation and focus more on prototyping and relying upon the code itself to act as the documentation. There is a lot of merit to this approach, but as of this writing it is still relatively new, with few examples of teams that do it effectively and consistently.

Tips for the Deliver Phase

- Details, details, details.
- Make a decision and move on.

Details, details, details.

A lack of details will break your design even if the direction and concept are solid. The detail work at this stage is where your craftsmanship and professionalism are reflected, and can make the difference between an acceptable product and a great one.

Make a decision and move on.

"Simply making decisions, one after another, can be a form of art."

- John Gruber

While it is important to fill in the details, that doesn't mean that every decision is design-altering. Less experienced designers (but sometimes even veterans) can often become obsessed over certain design choices. They will list all the pros and cons, analyze every choice, and test their designs to death but cannot bring themselves to make a final decision.

When it is time to make the final call some designers feel paralyzed because all of sudden their decision matters. Some designers panic when they realize their design decision will go into production and become a real thing in the real world for real people to use.

It is natural and maybe even a good thing for a UX Designer to feel some weight on their shoulders for that responsibility. Feeling this sense of responsibility will push you to do better. However, when it is time to make decisions you have to have the confidence to make a choice and move forward. And if you turn out to be wrong, you must acknowledge your mistakes and learn from them.

The Design Process and Product Development Lifecycle

This design process model described in this chapter depicts a high-level design process in isolation. In the real world, it is always intertwined with the larger product development lifecycle. Design happens in conjunction with the product manager's process and the engineering process, the product marketing process, and the sales process. This means that companies incorporate the design process into the product development lifecycle in different ways.

Some organizations have a high design maturity and know how to effectively incorporate UX Design, but some are still years away from figuring it out. In less mature product organizations, UX Design may be left completely out of the product development lifecycle until the very end. Every designer we know has a story about how they were asked to "fix" the UI of a product that had months of engineering development with no design input. If you couldn't have guessed, that does not result in well-designed products or happy UX Designers.

However, in organizations with high design maturity, the UX Designer works together with product management and engineering like a well-oiled machine from the very start and throughout all stages of the product lifecycle. The best way to incorporate the design process into other organizational processes always makes for a good debate, but it is encouraging to see that most companies are constantly trying to do it better.

UX Designers and managers can make this transition easier by ensuring that their design process is flexible enough to fit with other job functions. It is unreasonable to assume that UX Designers can have their ideal design process if it means forcing all other existing teams to adjust theirs. Incorporating different processes together means compromise. For a simple example, if a development team never worked with UX Designers before and it is their first time developing a UI from design specifications, for the first release the UX Designer might need to take on UI quality assurance responsibilities to help ensure the final product is up to the designer's standards.

For another example, if there is huge amount of back-end work for a new product, then the UX Designer might need to deliver early versions of work-in-progress wireframes so the software programming team can scope the work and start building a backend. UX Designers have to balance these compromises in a way that accounts for the realities of the organization while putting the user's experience ahead of other competing priorities.

4
Research
& Design
Methods

"The expectations of life depend upon diligence; the mechanic that would perfect his work must first sharpen his tools."

Confucius

UX Designers utilize many methods, some borrowed from other disciplines and some created within the UX discipline itself. While some methods such as user interviews may be considered to be more "research" than "design", we do not classify any method as such because all methods are by nature intertwined in UX practice. Good designers can leverage these methods in the design process as needed for the project.

Perhaps even more important than knowing how to use a method is knowing *when* to use the method. Each method has its own purpose and provides its own type of value at different times in the design process. Once you build fluency in these methods you will begin to see the pros and cons of each one, and will cultivate the judgment to know when and how to wield them in your projects.

Also, once you become familiar with them you should not limit yourself to rigid textbook descriptions. Feel free to modify them for your own unique challenges. You are encouraged to create your own methods, too.

What follows is a list of the most fundamental methods that all UX Designers should know how to use and also when to use them. Each method includes a rough primer with tips on how you can start using them in your projects. This list is intended to be a beginner's guide, as there are entire books written about these methods. And as always, there is no substitute for real-world practice.

Interview

In a nutshell, an interview is where you ask someone to answer a series of questions in their own words. Interviews are one of the most commonly used methods across many professions, not just by UX Researchers and Designers. The true art of it lies in how to effectively collect the information you need through a facilitated but loosely structured conversation. Interviews can stand alone as a separate research activity, or they can be incorporated into other methods and activities such as usability testing and contextual inquiry.

Preparing for the interview

Before you sit down with your interview participant, you should have a plan that covers what you want to know as well as the structure of the interview. You can take notes yourself, or record the interview if you get permission from the participant. To avoid complications, you should choose a recording method that you are accustomed to and the participant is comfortable with.

Conducting the interview

Generally speaking, most interview structures start with an introduction and a rundown of the topics that will be covered. Then you move on to a couple of quick, interesting, and easy-to-answer questions to get the participant comfortable and engaged. After that your overall question flow should go from generic to specific, and from easy to difficult. You should end with a couple more light and easy questions, and thank the participant for their time.

During the interview you should feel free to add and remove questions on the spot, and be flexible if the conversation deviates from the plan. Remember that the participant is offering their perspective on the topic, so even if the conversation is off the planned path you should give them the opportunity to express themselves. Often the best insights come from the unplanned portion of the interview.

The real art of the interview comes from knowing how to steer the conversation towards these insightful areas while staying on topic. Good researchers conduct themselves in a way that makes the participant feel relaxed, trusting, and willing to share honest thoughts. Some people are naturally good at this, but for most it takes practice.

Interview Questions

It is important to word your questions deliberately and appropriately. Without a doubt, the most common mistake people make while conducting interviews is to ask leading or biased questions. A leading question is one that skews the participant's response by implying that there is a "correct" or "more acceptable" answer. Here are a couple of examples of leading questions:

Example 1
LEADING
"Can you please describe how good you think this feature is?"

NON-LEADING
"Can you please tell me what you think about this feature?"

Example 2
LEADING
"Most of our users describe the product as easy to use. Do you think it is easy to use?"

NON-LEADING
"On a scale of 1 to 5, how would you rate the ease of use of this product?"

The non-leading question in Example 2 is typically made in a survey, but in an interview you can directly ask the participant to explain their rating. This can provide much more insight than relying solely on quantitative responses.

Group Interviews

Group interviews, also called focus groups, are conducted in much the same manner as individual interviews. When recruiting participants for a group interview, typically you want people from a similar social group to ensure open and honest feedback. For example you shouldn't put bosses and their employees in the same group since it can make the employees reluctant to answer truthfully.

Also, during a group interview a common problem occurs where one or two people end up doing most of the talking or controlling the pace or topic of conversation. Part of the facilitator's job is to ensure that everyone contributes to the discussion. One of the easiest ways to do this is to keep note of who isn't contributing much, address them by their name and ask, "What do you think?"

Contextual Inquiry

Contextual inquiry is a method created by Hugh Beyer and Karen Holtzblatt to collect data based on people's behavior by observing them in their normal situations, or even participating in their work or actions yourself. Contextual inquiry can be done at the beginning or the end of the product cycle. When conducted at the beginning of the product cycle you can get insight into what design direction might make the most sense. During the later stage of the product cycle, if you have a functioning prototype you can observe how the current product or your own design is used in the real context.

Contextual inquiry is great to combine with usability testing in the field. Your design may perform well in a usability lab with no distractions, but it might perform poorly in the real environment when the user is interrupted by people stopping at their desk or needing to answer their phone.

Preparation

Before you do anything you must have a clear profile of your target audience and the problem you are trying to solve. Then you can schedule the sessions with the appropriate people. Contextual inquiry sessions can be a few hours or even a full day, and it is imperative that you schedule a time when you can observe the user working in their natural context.

During contextual inquiry your role as researcher is to learn from users in their environment. While it is expected that you will ask questions, you should familiarize yourself with the vocabulary, topic, and work of the user's context. For instance, if you plan to observe animators to learn how they use computer drawing tools, you should study animation and movie technology ahead of time so you don't have to constantly ask for definitions. Instead you can pay attention to how the animator uses these words and tools in their normal work environment.

Conducting contextual inquiry

Like most other types of research, you should have an introduction and warm-up session with the people involved to restate the purpose of the study and set expectations. It is important that you set the expectation that you are there to learn from them in the real environment, not to help with their problems, answer their questions, or evaluate their work. Your priority is to be in-context to observe and learn at the side of the individual. This usually manifests in one of two types of relationships that you can form with the user.

The first is a master and apprentice relationship, where you are the apprentice observing the master (your user). The master's role is to focus on what she needs to do while narrating (to you) what she is doing and why. The second is a partnership in which you participate in the task together with the user. In this situation you discuss assumptions, details, purposes, methods, and better practices. You can choose one relationship type or mix them both according to your study's needs. Just remember that contextual inquiry relies on trust and integrity. You are not there to offer solutions, judge, teach, or sell.

What to look for

You should take notes on whatever is relevant to your research, but here are some common things to pay attention to:

- What is the environment like? What kind of energy or vibe does the place have? Is it relaxed, tense, noisy, boring, etc?

- What tools does the user interact with (including competitor products) and how do they use them?

- What is the user's personal method of doing things, and do they differ from other people?

- When and how does the user collaborate with other people? What is her relationship to these other people? Is she the director, boss, or facilitator? Or is she in more of a supporting role?

- Does she use printed reports, schedules, annotations, calendars, or Post-it notes? Ask permission to take photos or get copies of anything relevant.

Data analysis

Contextual inquiry tends to result in a large amount of scattered data. To make the data easier to deal with it is preferable to do the analysis as soon as your contextual inquiry session is done. Refer to the affinity diagramming method in this chapter, as it is a great method for analyzing this kind of data. At the end of your data analysis, you should refer back to your initial understanding prior to the contextual inquiry and see how your perspective or understanding has changed.

Survey

Interviews, focus groups, and contextual inquiry are great for learning about a small representative group of users. They are not so good at getting statistically valid descriptions about your user segments, and that is where surveys are so helpful. A survey is a list of arranged questions delivered to a large number of people.

The art of the survey lies in how to craft those questions to get valid and useful data. It is very easy to design a bad survey that results in unusable data, and even easier to design a survey that provides misleading data. To get good, usable data you have to consider what questions to ask, how to word them, and what type to use.

Surveys can be quickly deployed to find out a wealth of self-reported descriptive information such as how many of your users fit in a certain age group or what percentage of your product users are parents. Surveys can also be used along with other methods. It is very common to use a survey as the screening method to recruit only certain types of audiences for usability testing, interviews, or focus groups. The information collected by the survey then becomes part of your research data as profile information on your study participants.

Preparation

You need to establish a clear goal if you wish to create an effective survey. Are you trying to understand how satisfied users are about certain feature, or are you simply trying to get profile information of your audience? Once you have a clear goal you can then come up with a rough list of questions you would like to have answered.

With this rough list in hand, the next step is to write the survey. You must be careful to avoid leading questions, as mentioned in the section on Interviews. Besides that, here are a few additional tips for writing good survey questions:

- Keep the survey short.
- Use mostly close-ended questions.
- Pair open-ended questions with close-ended questions.
- Make questions specific, concise, and consistent.
- Avoid questions that require people to predict their own future behavior.
- Provide specific, appropriate answers to multiple-choice questions.
- Test your survey.

Keep the survey short.

People get "survey fatigue" after a few minutes, causing them to answer less genuinely later in the survey as they did at the beginning.

Use mostly close-ended questions.

Closed-ended questions are questions with a limited set of choices for the answers. For example you might ask, "Which of the following devices do you have in your house?" followed by a list of devices. Or you could ask them to rank a list of features from the most useful to the least useful. This makes it easier for the survey taker to complete the survey, as well as simplifying data analysis for you.

Pair open-ended questions with closed-ended questions.

Open-ended questions are questions where the user can answer freely in their own words. Since the answers are so unstructured, open-ended questions are hard to quantify if they aren't related to a closed-ended question. You should also make open-ended questions optional for the participant unless they are absolutely necessary for your study. Otherwise many survey participants will abandon the survey, or end up typing something unhelpful just to get past the question.

Make questions specific, concise, and consistent.

There will be noise in the data if users are confused about how to answer the questions or if the answers themselves create contradictions or confusion in the analysis.

Avoid questions that require people to predict their own future behavior.

Surveys are self-reported data. If you ask the question "Will you use this feature?" the survey participant is only telling you what they think they might do in the future. There is no guarantee that they indeed would use the feature. Instead, you might ask, "How interested are you in using this feature?" and provide choices like "very interested, somewhat interested, or not interested."

Provide specific, appropriate answers to multiple-choice questions.

The user can only pick from the answers provided, so make sure the answers fit the question, are specific and mutually exclusive to reduce confusion, and offer a selection thorough enough to apply to all users.

Test your survey.

After your survey is written, we highly recommend that you test the survey just like you would with a product design. Have a couple of people in your target audience take the survey and think out loud as you observe and listen. This way you can discover issues with poorly worded questions before sending it to a larger audience.

Distributing the survey

Today most surveys are distributed online for convenience and speed. There are many simple online survey tools such as Survey Monkey, Zoomerang, and Google Forms. Each of them has their own capabilities, pros, and cons so we encourage you to experiment with all of them to choose one that meets your needs.

There is rarely a reason to make a survey publicly available to everyone in the world. Make sure when sending out your survey that you control who gets an invitation to fill it out. If it is important that only your customers take the survey, don't send the links out to family and friends asking them to forward it along. This will create noise in the resulting data.

Data analysis

Nearly every online survey tool provides some kind of report that you can use for analysis. The following image shows a Google Forms survey report from a basic survey we conducted to gather information about certain board game players and their habits:

52 responses

View all responses   Publish analytics

Summary

How many board games do you own (including card games)?

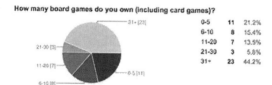

0-5	11	21.2%
6-10	8	15.4%
11-20	7	13.5%
21-30	3	5.8%
31+	23	44.2%

How often do you play board games?

less than 1-3 times a month	13	25%
1-3 times a month	17	32.7%
1-2 times a week	17	32.7%
more than 2 times a week	5	9.6%

Who do you play board games with?

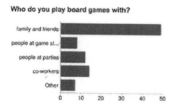

family and friends	49	94.2%
people at game stores	8	15.4%
people at parties	12	23.1%
co-workers	14	26.9%
Other	7	13.5%

Survey data analysis is a complex domain unto itself, but in many cases most of the important things can be revealed using basic analysis methods. Remember that as a UX Designer, the research is there to produce timely insights to serve design. Survey analysis doesn't mean you have to mine the data to discover every possible insight. You only need to discover the insights necessary to produce design work. With that in mind, here are some basic analysis techniques to start with.

First of all, take a step back and revisit your goals. Read a couple of survey responses just to get a sense of how people answered the survey and what the answers reveal about your goals. Next, since most of your questions should have been closed-ended you can look for trends by simply counting how many and what percentage of people chose each option. This can help you say something like "40 percent of our users indicated they use this tool 2 hours per day", which may be a simple but very valuable insight.

Another simple but powerful analysis method is cross-tabulation. It is used to group data based on answers and then compare to another set of answers to find relationships. For example, you might have the following two questions in your survey:

1. What is your age?
[ ] 21 or less
[ ] 22-35
[ ] 36-55
[ ] 56 or more

2. Which of the following features did you find the most valuable?
[ ] Feature A
[ ] Feature B
[ ] Feature C

With cross-tabulation you can see if there is a correlation between people's age and what feature they found the most valuable.

Age Group	Feature A		Feature B		Feature C		Total	
21 or less	100	66.7%	22	14.67%	28	18.67%	150	25%
22 - 35	75	50%	29	19.33%	46	30.67%	150	25%
36-55	24	12%	160	80%	16	8%	200	33%
56 or more	17	17%	24	24%	59	59%	100	17%
Total	216	36%	235	39.17%	149	24.83%	600	

As you can see in the above example, out of 200 people in the age group of 36-55, 80% reported that they found Feature B the most valuable. On the other hand, within 150 people in age group of 21 or less only 15% of them reported that they found Feature B the most valuable. It may be of design interest to understand why Feature B strongly resonates with one age group but not another.

Statistical Significance

As a final note about survey analysis, there are varying opinions regarding what makes a survey statistically significant. Depending on the size and diversity of your target audience, you could need as few as 10 responses or as many as 1,000. There are several "statistical significance" calculators you can use to identify what you need, but like so many things in UX Design it comes down to your judgement.

In summary, understand that surveys describe the whole by sampling a subset that is assumed to be a proxy for the whole group. There are always other factors that affect the confidence of your conclusions, such as the quality of your questions or that people might not be truthful in their answers for various reasons.

Affinity Diagram

You can quickly accumulate a large amount data after just a couple of research activities. Affinity Diagramming is a great method for cleaning up and organizing a large amount of disparate data points so that trends and insights can be discovered from within the chaos.

Preparation

Collect all your research data into one place by gathering all recordings, notes, and artifacts. Then write down one singular data point or observation on a Post-it note. We highly recommend yellow for readability. When creating these data points it is common to have similar or duplicated ones, especially if there are multiple people on your team doing this.

Find a large flat surface such as a wall, whiteboard, or window. You and your team group notes into clusters that are related to each other, one note at a time. Each team member can talk about how they relate in their minds, but it doesn't really matter as long as all of you feel they relate. Try to keep each cluster between 2 to 4 Post-it notes. However, this is only a general rule. It is possible that there is no good way to break them into such small groups.

After the initial clustering is done, give each cluster a label or summary on a Post-it note colored differently from the first (such as blue). Next, identify how many individual orange Post-it notes there are, which now represent the clusters. If there are too many to logically process your group should then organize the orange clusters into another level of clusters, giving them a label with a third color of Post-it notes.

ORDER FREQUENCY	TOOLS USED	APPROVAL PATHS	USER LOCATION	USER PERCEPTION
Jill answers the phone at least 10 times / day	Jill uses Excel to organize all orders	Jill's draft must be approved by Xuan before it is accessible to Thomas	Jill sits next to Thomas	Rob perceives that the system works like an assembly line
Rob needs to order supplies twice / week	Order approval and order Submission are separate systems	Rob must ask his boss for permission each time he orders supplies	Xuan is in a different building than Jill, Thomas, and Rob	

Once you have organized all the Post-it notes, you will have a layered structure of all data points. From there you can easily summarize insights and discover trends across all your data. The previous image shows what a very small finished affinity diagram looks like. However, affinity diagrams usually consist of dozens if not hundreds of notes.

Card Sort

Card Sorting is a method to reveal how people perceive and organize information by having them sort a collection of cards with labels written on them. This is a common method for designing the information architecture for apps and websites. This method is used when you know what information to include and who the intended audience is, but before having ways to organize and navigate the info.

Preparation

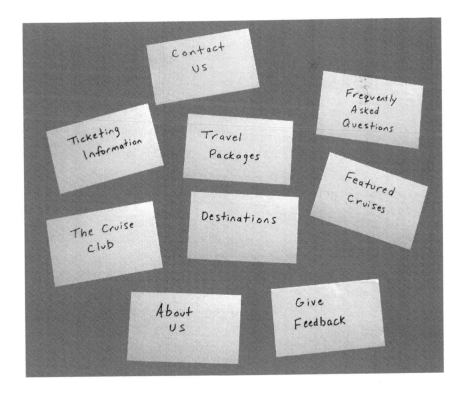

Write down one topic, concept, or piece of information relevant to your project on separate pieces of paper or cards. Most people use index cards, but you can use any type of cards as long as they are the same size and style. You should have one set of cards for each user you plan to conduct a card sort with.

The previous image shows an example set of cards you might use if you were designing a cruise travel website. For clarity each topic should be clearly understood on its own, but if a certain topic requires explanation you can write a brief description on the card itself. Each topic should have an appropriate granular level and reflect what you want to find out.

For example, you might have company history, mission statement, leadership, and investor information that you feel belongs under "About Us". In this situation you might provide cards for each of those to see how your users perceive them and organize them. You can even have images or quotes on the cards. It all depends on what you want to find out.

Conducting a card sort

You should conduct card sorting sessions with one user from your target audience at a time, with about 4-10 sessions as a minimum. Use a location with a large flat surface at a comfortable height (conference rooms with large tables are great), and have all the cards on the table when the participant arrives. Don't put them in any particular order. The more random the better since you don't want to suggest any predetermined order.

When it is time to start the card sorting session, make sure to convey the following to each card sort participant:

- Set the context by describing what the product, service, or website is about.

- Introduce the card sorting exercise to them. If space permits, ask the participant to sort the cards without stacking them. This way you can see every card in a group.

- Remind them that not every card has to be grouped. If something feels like it doesn't belong they are free to leave it out.

- Encourage them to focus on what makes sense to them, and that there is no right or wrong way to organize.

- Ask them to think out loud as they sort, freely ask questions, and seek clarification as needed.

Once the participant is finished organizing the cards, ask them to label the groups using Post-it notes. (Asking them to label after they group ensures they group based on their initial instincts, not on predetermined labels.) When they are done labeling, bind the cards and the group labels together with rubber bands or binder clips. If there are lots of groups you can ask the participant to group more levels and label them as well.

Analysis

Lay out all participants' card groups on a large surface. Look through the groups one by one first. You will notice trends of how different participants grouped the cards. Then you can focus on one card at a time to see how the same index card was put in different or similar groups by different participants. Pay close attention to the cards people didn't find good groups for. They may represent a topic or feature that is confusing or perhaps doesn't belong in the site or app.

Note that the groups reveal how people relate the concepts, not how they want to or should navigate them. While card sorting can inform the navigation for your site or app, you can't just take a group of cards and directly create information architecture from it.

Participatory Design

Participatory design is an activity in which your users are invited to actively participate in the creative process. Sessions can be done with individuals or as a group activity. Participants are typically given tasks to design the best tools or environment for themselves. Their mental models, motivation, desires, fears, and opinions are revealed through their design ideas and thought processes.

Preparation

Before the session you should recruit a small number of your target audience, typically 2-5 people. Prepare design tasks, design materials, and design inspiration for the participants to engage with.

Design tasks

This is what you will be asking the participants to do during the session. For example, if you are designing a recipe organization tool the design task for your participants might be to "Create a recipe organization book that best fits your needs."

Design materials

Provide materials that are easy for anyone to pick up and create with such as paper, pens, pencils, Post-it notes, tape, rubber bands, paper clips, scissors, and stickers. Provide an abundance of them since you never know how much your participants will use. It is much better to have leftover unused materials than not enough.

Design inspiration

These are items that help trigger creative thinking such as posters, color wheels, illustrations, cartoons, icons, different shapes, motifs, or patterns in addition to things that are specific to the design task. For example, participatory design for a recipe organization tool might include recipe books, recipe cards, or images of food and kitchens.

Conducting a participatory design session

Choose a location where you can create an informal and relaxed environment that helps the flow of creativity. Ideally you would choose a place with windows and lots of open space. For the recipe organization tool example, you might even consider conducting your participatory design session in a real kitchen.

Explain to all participants what the design task is, and make it very clear that they are designing for themselves and shouldn't worry about what their friends, family, or anyone else would think about it. Give them plenty of time to get started, since it can take a while for some people to get their creativity going.

Pay attention to how the participants are engaged with the task. Just because someone isn't actively drawing or writing doesn't mean they are done. Most importantly, give them plenty of encouragement as needed but don't interrupt them during their own creative process.

After the design tasks are finished, ask the participant to explain their ideas. If you are conducting a group participatory session, allow each participant to explain how their idea works. Your job is to ask probing questions and facilitate discussion to glean an understanding of their thought process.

The actual design ideas may or may not be good or useful, but that isn't the point of participatory design. The process and final artifacts reveal a lot about the users: their logic, motivations, desires, emotions, mental models, as well as their own tips and tricks, metaphors they use for meaning making, workflows suggested by the design, and the desired relationship between themselves and the tool.

Personas

You may have piles of data about your users, but if you consider their needs on an individual level it is just too overwhelming and unfeasible to design for each person individually. One effective way to have all data make sense and effectively inform your thinking is to build models of users and people based on the data. These models are called personas.

A persona is a synthesized individual that represents a group of users. It is only a model, not a real person, but it is personified with attributes of a real person such as age, gender, desires, motivations, goals, and fears. Creating personas helps the product team to have a shared understanding of who the users are, which is critical for making decisions as a team. Personas also help you come up with new ideas and validate those ideas by helping you put yourself in their shoes. Without a persona to reference, our natural tendency is to design towards our own needs instead of the user's.

However, when you are designing for a persona named "Sophie" you can ask yourself simple questions like "What will Sophie do in this situation?" or "Will Sophie like this idea?" This will help you think of other ideas you would not have otherwise, or discard ideas that clearly go against Sophie's needs.

The following images are just a couple of examples of how personas can be documented and the kinds of information that they may include.

Mitchell Straus
Lighting Artist, 36 years old

Primary Work Goals

1. Create realistic lighting that is powerful and emotive

2. Have a workflow for finishing shots quickly

"All visual impressions on the viewer depend on proper lighting."

"The tool is just a means to an end. An important means, but still just a tool."

"I need to work quickly and precisely."

Background and Story

Mitchell started at Pixar, and came to Disney Animation at the end of Bolt. Having been at Pixar he is acutely aware of the cultural and processural differences between the two studios. He wants the tools and processes to be designed better, and to bridge the disconnect between artists and developers. However, he is inclined to believe that developers should come to him. He isn't particularly confident that TW is the answer, but he is willing to give it a try.

He spends most of this time inside of Pix and Light, among other tools. He is frustrated that he has to stop working on a shot just to go looking for documentation. If and when he ever finds it, he is disappointed that there is not much about workflow. He has taken it upon himself in several situations to share his workflow with other lighters, and frequently works with Joseph (TD) to improve their workflow, fix bugs, and get things done.

He finds tech demos useful and likes knowing about the cutting edge stuff coming out of the technical department. He is very savvy with the current tools, and using them has become second nature to him. He is willing to learn new things if they make his workflow faster. He cares about the shot most of all, and has no loyalty to any tool. However, he also has a threshold for how much bugginess he will deal with before going back to the more stable versions.

Entry points to the system

- Looking for most recent feature updates, likely through RSS or email notification
- Frequently changes versions of software, so expects to be able to easily find version-related documents
- Searching for software demos, videos, and tutorials
- Contributing to forums where artists ask questions
- After using the "Help" in the tool itself, looking elsewhere for needed information
- Looking for developer working on the tool

What will prevent him using the system?

- There are no videos
- There are no other artists using it to communicate and collaborate
- The content is outdated, half-finished, and not version-controlled
- Search doesn't work and he can't find information quickly
- No screenshots to identify what he is looking at
- No community around artistic side of things

Sophie Kelly
Director of UX Research & Analytics
shoelovers.com

Her job
- Research & understand visitor behavior, needs, and feedback
- Identify areas of improvement about online experience and make suggestions

What does she use this product for?
- drafting, building, launching online surveys
- analyzing survey responses for business and design

Pain points

Very slow performance   Buggy UI

Limited question types

Poor reporting & analysis features

Photo by Steve Wilson, CC 2.0

Product Use

Understand
Analyze ← → Share
Influence

Excel
Google Forms
Survey Monkey

Survey & Analysis

Google Analytics
Site Catalyst
Flurry

Site Analytics

75

Creating personas

There are countless opinions about how to create personas, and different situations call for different approaches. In this book our goal is to provide universal tips on how to build good design personas that should work in the majority of situations:

> - Ground your personas with your research.
> - Avoid personas that are too generic.
> - Avoid personas that are too specific.
> - Include information based on the needs of the project.
> - Make persona artifacts concise, clear, and focused.

Ground your personas with research.

Personas should be grounded in your research data. Comb through all your data again before constructing personas. You can use your judgment and educated assumptions to fill some gaps, but don't make major unsupported claims.

Avoid personas that are too generic.

For example, if you are designing a website for a university, international prospective students and domestic prospective students would likely require that you create two separate personas. Each type of student is likely to have very different needs and motivations, and they may even have different admission procedures.

Avoid personas that are too specific.

Conversely, you must avoid personas that are too specific. Using the previous university website example, when considering international prospective students it might not make sense to have an Asian prospective student persona in addition to a European prospective student persona. One "foreign student" persona may be enough.

Include information based on the needs of the project.

Start by focusing on what is relevant and necessary. Imagine you are designing a photo organization tool and the persona is a 35-year-old stay-at-home mom. While it may help to round out the personality of the persona, there isn't much design value in describing what time she gets up or when she drops the kids off at school. That information might be helpful if you were designing a daily schedule management tool, but for a photo organization tool it is likely just noise.

Make persona artifacts concise, clear, and focused.

Your design personas won't be effective if they don't get adopted by others, and they won't get adopted by others if they are not understood. It is important to have persona documentation that can quickly and easily be accessed and understood by people outside the design team.

There are many different ways to represent personas, and some design teams get very creative with them. Some teams create cards, flyers, books, websites, and posters. No matter how you choose to represent the persona we recommend that you have at least one type of persona document where all the content can fit on a single page. Utilize a nice layout with clean typography. Include simple graphics and charts to make it easier to scan, read, and digest.

Using personas in design

It is a waste of effort to create nice persona sheets or graphics just to keep them to yourself. Personas are great for designers, but they are even better for everyone else involved in the project. It is best to print out your persona materials and display them in the physical environment for easy reference by the whole team throughout the project. Bring the persona artifacts to your design brainstorms, design reviews, and critique sessions. Refer to them if there is a debate about who the target users are or what they would want.

Now, even though we have said a lot about the benefits of personas, it is important to understand their weaknesses. Personas should not be taken too literally or relied upon too heavily. Sometimes risk-averse product teams fall into the trap of trying to validate every single idea against the persona out of fear of making mistakes or trying to absolve themselves of decision-making responsibilities.

This is bad practice. While personas can probably help you validate some ideas when you imagine how the persona would interact using the design, they do not hold any magic standards that all ideas can be tested against. Personas are useful for inspiration and direction, and occasionally validation, but never as a substitute for common sense and good judgment.

Flow Diagrams

A flow diagram is a graphical representation of how the elements within a system sequentially relate to or interact with each other. The interaction design aspect of UX Design can't be done without creating some kind of flow diagram, since the user's experience takes place over time and typically requires some kind of decision making.

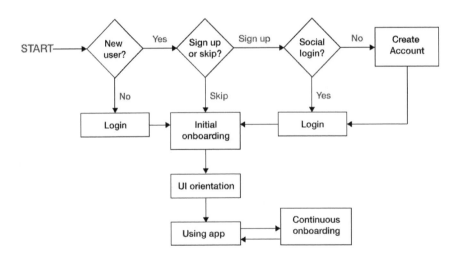

UX Designers use flow diagrams for many different reasons as part of the design process. Sometimes they are used to communicate a comprehensive overview of how the system works. Other times they are used to describe task or screen flows to illustrate how each use case is handled, where there are opportunities to teach or delight, and where friction points might occur. The previous image shows an example of a flow diagram for a simple setup experience. You could take a diagram like that and easily use it as the basis for a storyboard or prototype.

Flow diagrams are also a common artifact for use with development teams and product managers because they show all the paths and flows in one diagram. This helps to better plan how to build the system to cover every use case since it illustrates where users will need to make decisions, where errors might occur, and what part of the system has a dependency upon something else.

Creating flow diagrams

There are many different ways to create flows, and there is no true right or wrong way to do it. However, there are two pretty universal rules when it comes to creating flow diagrams:

> 1. Have goals for the user. These goals may be purely user goals, but often are also product or system goals such as "successfully filled out profile information" or "made a purchase."

> 2. Describe how the user enters and ends the flow. Ideally, they end the flow when they have completed their goal.

UX Designers use dozens of tools and techniques to create flow diagrams. As part of the sketching process, many UX Designers just use pen and paper or a whiteboard. Just like sketching, this method is fast, organic, and easy to do as a group. However, these diagrams aren't always easy to share with others. If you frequently need to share with others or create documentation it can be preferable to use software.

Some of the most popular desktop software tools for creating diagrams are Microsoft Visio (not available on Mac) and Omnigraffle (only available on Mac). Some of the most popular web-based tools are Gliffy, Draw.io, and Lucid Charts. While none of these tools was created specifically for UX Designers, each of them offers what you need: symbols, templates, and the ability to connect lines and arrows to other diagram elements. This makes it much easier to change and move around elements of the diagram without breaking flows.

Storyboards

Storyboards, also known as narratives or scenarios, are a method to articulate how a certain experience unfolds. Storyboards are typically constructed much like comic book panels to tell a story, often with personas as the characters. Since storyboards depict people and situations instead of features, you often get more relevant design feedback from your audience about persona needs instead of the audience's own personal feelings.

Storyboards are often used to tell the story of existing products to articulate the overall experience and identify areas of improvement. However, storyboards are at their most useful when used to imagine an ideal version of how the experience can be. There are many ways to do this, but typically they are high-level, contextual storyboards that focus on a persona's motivations and needs and how the product can help, empower, enrich, and in general provide something positive to the persona. The goal of this type of storyboard is to create a clear, concrete experiential goal for the product to strive towards.

For instance, in the following example the main persona is hungry but doesn't want to wait in the long line. He remembers that there is an app where he can order his food, and after just a few minutes he gets an alert that his order is ready. He skips the line, grabs his food, and is on his way before the line even moved.

While very simple in nature, the example shows how in just a few panels (and with rudimentary drawing skills) you can convey a concept, interaction, and experience.

Constructing the storyboard

Constructing a storyboard is just like telling any story. You need to know who the characters are, when and where the story takes place, what objects are involved, and what happens during the story. There should be a beginning, middle, and end resulting in a clear, convincing resolution to the character's needs or desires. Use your imagination and strive for the best experience possible for the characters.

Rendering the storyboard

Storyboards require drawing, but you don't need to be an amazing illustrator to create a storyboard. There are even storyboarding tools that have pre-made characters and scenes. No matter what you use to create the final artifact, your storyboards will come out much better if you sketch all of them first. If drawing feels too intimidating or you don't know where to start, try writing your stories down as if you were writing the script to a play or movie. Once you have your story ready, break it down into scenes that can serve as the basis for your panels.

For each panel, read the scene and decide on the key elements to include. Which character or characters belong in the scene? Should you include their whole body or is it enough to include just hands or head? What objects are necessary and where should they be? How does your character communicate? With speech or thought bubbles, or with facial expressions?

If you find that a particular panel is too complicated break it down into more panels. Keep it simple. Unless you are already a great comic artist, you will find it easier to put in only the minimum necessary elements. It will help the audience to focus on the important parts of the story and will make it easier for you to draw. If there are certain elements you are not sure how to draw, do a quick Internet image search of that object to get inspiration.

Characters are typically the hardest element to draw, but you don't need to draw them in realistic form. Abstract simple human forms such as star figures and stick figures can be sufficient. The same applies to other elements, too. If a simple form can convey what the element is you don't need to make it realistic.

In Deb Aoki's "On the Same Page" presentation about simple sketching and storyboarding, she provides great examples of how easy it is to draw people, objects, and perspectives for your storyboards:

CIRCLE + SQUARE + DOTS + LINES = PEOPLE!

ADD A FEW TWEAKS = DIFFERENT PEOPLE

CIRCLE + DOTS + LINES = FACES AND EMOTIONS

WORD BALLONS ... WITHOUT WORDS

DRAW COMMON CONCEPTS IN A FEW STROKES

CONNECT CONCEPTS WITH LINES

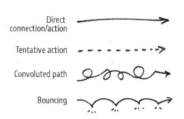

DIFFERENT PERSPECTIVES OF USER INTERACTION

CLOSE-UP
Emphasis on
screen/finger interaction

SEMI-CLOSE
Emphasis on device/
human context/use

MID-TORSO
Emphasis on screen

FULL BODY
Emphasis on 'real world'
context/place of use

images used courtesy of Deb Aoki: www.slideshare.net/DebAoki/storyboarding-csa2013

Wireframing

Wireframes are one of the most common artifacts that UX Designers create. Wireframes are representations of a user interface that include only lines, shapes, and text to convey the layout and elements of UI. They can be made many ways, but they often include the actual size and dimensions of the UI and are typically made purposefully devoid of color to not be confused with the exact visual design.

The actual fidelity of a wireframe can vary, but the main goal is to help the designer focus on what elements are included in the interface and how the product works instead of how it looks. Wireframes can communicate design in many ways when combined with storyboards, prototypes, and specifications.

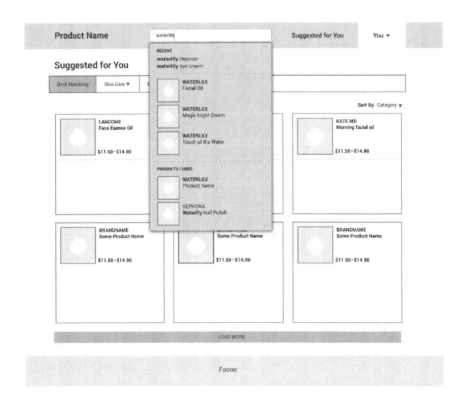

Wireframing tools

While you can easily create wireframes with pen and paper, most jobs prefer that UX Designers use one of many software tools available. Here we will discuss a few we have personally used and that are fairly common in the industry: Balsamic Mockups, Adobe Illustrator, Adobe Fireworks, Sketch, and Omnigraffle. If you are just starting out we highly recommend trying these tools so you can benefit from the wealth of online education resources as well as the shared asset libraries created by designers from all around the world.

Balsamic Mockups

Balsamiq Mockups is fast and lightweight, and is probably the easiest tool to learn because it was created solely for UI designers to make wireframes and low-fidelity mockups. It allows you to create wireframes that look like sketches while still giving you control over sizes and dimensions. The website has very good tutorials for you to get started.

Adobe Illustrator

Adobe Illustrator is a vector-based illustration tool but it can also be used as a wireframing tool. However, since it is not mainly for UI design, if you aren't already familiar with it you may find it has a steeper learning curve compared to other tools. Despite the complexity, Adobe Illustrator is commonly used as a wireframing tool because it provides a lot of precision, is tightly integrated with other Adobe tools, and allows you to create final visual graphics from your wireframe file.

Adobe Fireworks

Adobe Fireworks is a vector and raster graphics editor intended to help web designers do pretty much everything in one tool. While there are very few people who use it as intended (prompting Adobe to stop development in 2013), it is still a good option for creating wireframes. If you can get past the learning curve, Fireworks is valuable for creating precise wireframes that can easily be converted into clickable prototypes.

Sketch

Sketch is a tool created solely for UI designers as a light-weight alternative to using complex graphics applications like Adobe Illustrator and Adobe Photoshop. If you have experience with other graphics software you will find Sketch to be very intuitive. It allows you to quickly create precise wireframes that can be turned into the final visual graphics.

Omnigraffle

Omnigraffle is a Mac-only application for creating diagrams but it has become a very popular tool for wireframing. Its popularity comes mainly from the large amount of quality, easy-to-use stencils available. Also, since it is a diagramming tool it is easy to create wireframes, flow diagrams, and design specifications all in the same document.

Prototyping

In UX Design a prototype is the model of a design that mimics the intended interactions. There are many different types of prototyping methods from low-fidelity paper prototypes, to medium-fidelity click-through wireframe prototypes, to high-fidelity prototypes made with code or special prototyping software. There are many benefits and uses for prototypes:

Prototypes for user testing

It is much cheaper to build a prototype and discover usability problems prior to building the system, as opposed to building something and then trying to fix problems in the production code.

Prototypes as tools for ideation

During the process of making the prototype designers can discover problems in the design that are harder to see in a static format. Similar to the benefits of pencil sketching, the creation of a prototype facilitates thinking and helps generate more ideas.

Prototypes as tools for communication

Prototypes are powerful to communicate design intention because they show people how it works. People don't have to imagine or read written descriptions, eliminating misinterpretation and saving time.

General prototyping principles

There are literally hundreds of books, blogs, and articles already written about prototyping. Over the course of a designer's career they learn and employ a variety of prototyping methods that work best for them. While there really is no "right" way to prototype, there are some fairly general and common prototyping principles that work for almost all UX Design processes:

> - Don't waste time crafting a perfect prototype.
> - Be flexible with your tools, techniques, media, and methods.
> - Strive for minimum-viable prototypes.
> - Don't be afraid to change the design.

Don't waste time crafting a perfect prototype.

Prototypes are intended to model a portion of the experience, not to be a substitute for the real thing.

Be flexible with your tools, media, and methods.

During your design career you will encounter different design processes, each at different stages with unique audiences who will require unique prototype formats. You should master a range of prototyping skills that cover different tools and techniques.

Strive for minimum-viable prototypes.

You should only prototype the minimum needed to convey the design, test, and get feedback. If you find that prototyping the interaction you need is too much work, find a way to fake it or mimic it.

Don't be afraid to change the design.

It is natural for your ideas and thoughts on the design to change when you are working on a prototype. Incorporate those changes into the prototype and see where they take you.

Deciding what to prototype

Assuming you have some design ideas sketched or wireframed already, next you should think about what you want to gain through prototyping to decide what aspects you should prototype. For example, imagine you are designing a shopping cart checkout experience and want to get a general feel for how long it will take the user to complete. In this case you could probably just prototype the most common path, making interactive elements for choosing an item and entering the shipping address and payment information. However, you probably wouldn't need to make interactive form elements for modifying item quantity or entering promotion codes.

Alternately, if you are prototyping the same design to be used in usability testing and one of the tasks for the user is to modify the item quantity, then that UI element would need to be interactive. Ultimately, there is no single "right" way to prototype, but there are some common starting points. Remember that a prototype is a tool that can be used for validation, ideation, and communication. Ask yourself why you are making the prototype and choose a prototyping fidelity and method that corresponds to your needs.

Deciding how to make your prototype

There are many ways to make prototypes, utilizing all kinds of different media, softwares, and techniques. In most instances you should choose the prototyping method that fits your goals and situation the best while requiring the least effort. Here are some things to consider when deciding how to make your prototype:

- What is the proper fidelity and material?
- What software and tools are you familiar with?
- How much time or budget do you have?
- Who is the audience for the prototype?

What is the proper fidelity and material?

This all depends on what you are trying to accomplish with the prototype. If you just need feedback on a basic flow perhaps you only need a paper prototype with rough sketches. If you are trying to communicate to the developer how to animate the transitions between screens you might need to create a video or slideshow. If you need to conduct usability testing you might want to create a fully interactive prototype.

What software and tools are you familiar with?

If you don't know how to code you can easily link screenshots together using tools like Adobe Fireworks or InVision. On the other hand, if you are good at front-end coding it might be easier for you to code the prototype instead.

How much time or budget do you have?

If you have lots of time and a budget, maybe you can purchase or learn a new tool that is the most appropriate for your prototype. If not you have to make do with what you have, which will be better than not prototyping at all.

Who is the audience for the prototype?

If you are building a prototype to get feedback on a basic flow maybe a paper prototype or simple black and white set of wireframes will be sufficient. On the other hand, if you try using something that informal to sell the design internally to a group of important decision makers it will not go over well. In that situation you may be better off creating an impressive high-fidelity prototype with polished visual design and full interactions, animations, and transitions.

Prototyping Tools

There are many tools used for prototyping. Here we list a sampling of prototyping tools that represent the full range of effort and interactive fidelity. The tool you choose should be based upon what you need to learn, the resources you have available, and your own technical skills.

Paper

low effort, low interactive fidelity

Paper is one of the quickest and most versatile ways to prototype interactions. The medium encourages honest feedback due to the engaging yet low-fidelity presentation. You can change the prototype in seconds with just another piece of paper. However, paper prototypes are hard to transport and are pretty much impossible to use in remote feedback sessions.

InVision

low effort, medium interactive fidelity

InVision is a web application that lets you import all your screens and link them together using clickable hotspots and animated transitions. It is especially good for mobile prototyping, and you can easily share the prototype with others and gather feedback. It probably has the most intuitive and lightweight workflow out of all the tools, and they have excellent documentation and tutorials in case you need help.

POP

low effort, medium interactive fidelity

POP app is a mobile application that is intended to let you work in pen and paper sketches and quickly turn them into a prototype using only your phone. If you just want to go from sketches to rough mobile prototype quickly, currently there is no better option than POP.

Adobe Fireworks

medium effort, medium interactive fidelity

Adobe Fireworks can also produce click-through prototypes like InVision, but you produce the prototype locally by linking hotspots across screens. This can be very efficient if you are already using Fireworks for wireframes and visual design. Fireworks can export everything into HTML files you can later host and distribute yourself (although the conversion to HTML isn't production-quality code).

Microsoft PowerPoint, Apple Keynote

medium effort, medium interactive fidelity

Both of these two presentation softwares allow you to easily produce click-through prototypes by linking slides together. You can't make a complex flow with them, but for simple flows they work great. You can also use their robust slide animation features to create UI transitions and animations. Keynote in particular has a lot of prototyping templates and tutorials made available by other designers.

Axure

high effort, high interactive fidelity

Axure is a very sophisticated prototyping tool typically used by large companies. It allows you to create nearly any interaction imaginable without needing to code, and automatically generates annotations and specifications. However, it is not easy to learn and is quite expensive.

Code

high effort, high interactive fidelity

If you are comfortable working with HTML, CSS, and Javascript you might find it most effective to prototype directly in a web browser. This is obviously the most high-fidelity, and you can prototype anything. If you use frameworks like Framer and jQuery Mobile you can easily create browser-based mobile prototypes as well.

Visual Mockups

Visual mockups are representations of a user interface that, unlike wireframes, are intended to show exactly how the final product should look. Many organizations have dedicated visual designers to handle this work, but in most jobs UX Designers are expected to do at least some mockup work. Often a visual designer can provide UI assets or templates, but at the very least you should be familiar with the common graphic design tools used in the industry.

Visual mockup tools

By far the most common tools for producing pixel-perfect visual mockups are Adobe Illustrator and Adobe Photoshop. Adobe Illustrator is very convenient for creating assets needed for responsive design since it is vector-based tool and can easily output different sizes for devices. Illustrator is sufficient for flat-looking graphics, but not so good for producing textures or complex visual elements.

Adobe Photoshop on the other hand is good at producing complex visual effects and textures. Adobe Photoshop is a bitmap-based tool, so the file size gets significantly larger when you have lots of elements in the file. It is also not very easy to produce different sizes for the same asset.

Like many other tools used in the industry, neither tool was solely intended to be used for UI design. This means there are hundreds of features you will likely never use, and the learning curve is very high for both of them. Regardless, you should still become familiar with them as they will likely remain the industry standard for graphic design tools for the foreseeable future.

However, there are tools like Sketch that are now being created specifically for UI designers. Sketch is intended to be a tool that only includes the best and most common features of Illustrator and Photoshop while adding in handy features for modern web and mobile design.

Usability Testing

Usability testing is a core user-centered design method used to uncover specific issues with how a product works, typically related to ease of use, learnability, or overall intuitiveness. It involves asking target users to complete a series of tasks using a prototype (or sometimes the real product), revealing usability problems through observation, listening, and asking questions.

It is important to conduct usability testing as early as possible to minimize cost and waste, preferably using a prototype and before any production code has been committed. It is almost pointless to test committed code because even if major issues are found, product teams may be reluctant to make any changes.

Usability testing can be a grand formal endeavor done with dozens of recruited participants in a sophisticated usability lab, or it can be very informal with friends using a paper prototype in a coffee shop. Tests are typically conducted in person but they can be done remotely as well. Remote tests are usually conducted over the phone with screen sharing software, but there are also third-party user research services like UserZoom that help you test remotely without the need of a facilitator.

There is no strict or standard way to conduct usability tests. Like many design methods it all depends on your organization, what you are trying to achieve, and the resources you have available to you. For example, when you have some early concepts you might want to do some "quick and dirty" testing with friends just using some wireframes and only focusing on high-level navigation or the most common tasks. Later on when you are deeper into the design and have a working prototype, you might want more formal testing to reveal comprehensive issues.

If you are short on time and budget, you might only get to test one small part of the design. Then you might have to decide between testing the most important part of the application to ensure you have solved the problem, or testing a part you are not confident about to get feedback so you can iterate on it.

Recruiting participants

Recruit participants that match with your target audience profile. For example, if you are designing a new eCommerce site that sells Asian-styled apparel for teenagers then your target users might be boys and girls from ages 12 to 18. In this situation you wouldn't include your grandfather in the user test group because he doesn't match the demographic. (Unless for some reason he regularly purchases Asian-styled apparel for young people, then maybe you could learn a lot from his unique perspective!)

Planning tasks

Write down the specific tasks you want the users to do in the study, focusing on areas of the design you want to test. Make sure to provide the user with context and clearly describe what they should do.

For example, imagine you are working on a web service called Textbook Jungle where students can rent or buy textbooks. For this usability test you want to test the flow for how to buy a particular textbook. You might write the following task for the user:

> "Next semester you are taking 'Human-Computer Interaction 101' and each student is required to have the textbook named The UX Learner's Guidebook by authors Camara and Zhao. You need to find all the buying options available to you on textbookjungle.com.
>
> Please start from the homepage of textbookjungle.com and find all options for acquiring that textbook for next semester."

Next you might create additional tasks to test other parts of the service such as returning or reserving a book.

The way you write the tasks can have a significant impact on how the test participant perceives and performs the tasks. A poorly worded task can cause a user to fail to complete the task even if there is no usability problem. (In that situation the usability issue is with the task, not the interface or product!) Here are a few tips for writing good usability study tasks:

- Provide context.

- Keep tasks simple and specific.

- Keep tasks focused on what you need to learn.

Provide context.

Each task should provide enough context to the user for them to understand why he or she is performing the task. Refer to the previous example, where the test participant is informed that they are a student taking a class and that they need to purchase a book specifically for that class.

Keep tasks simple and specific.

It is better to have the user go through several simple and specific tasks than a single complex task. If you must combine smaller tasks into one task make sure they are related.

Keep tasks focused on what you want to learn.

You can't test everything, so you have to prioritize. If your primary goal is to test the effectiveness of the purchase flow, don't ask the user to perform the task "Change your password." If the user can't figure out how to make a purchase it won't matter that your test showed how easily they could change a password.

Preparing the prototype

Prototypes intended for usability testing should place a priority on what you want to learn. If you are only testing the general web page flow, you could probably get by with paper prototypes or clickable wireframes. It would be a waste of time and effort to build a fully functional prototype. On the other hand, if you are looking for usability issues in a flow involving item selection, form fields, and system feedback you would be better off creating at least a semi-functional prototype.

Base the prototype on the usability task list you have. Even if you build a functional prototype it doesn't have to include every interaction and screen state. You always have limited time and resources so the prototype should only include enough functionality to cover the tasks you want the user to accomplish.

Conducting the usability testing session

Like any other research method that directly involves participants, there should always be an introduction to the study. During the introduction it is critical to explain that the product is the subject being tested, not the participant. This is important because you want participants to feel comfortable providing their honest feedback. Encourage them to voice their thoughts or concerns freely or abandon any tasks they can't complete.

Explain the "think-aloud" protocol, which is to have the participant think out loud while performing tasks. Instruct the participant to voice what they are looking at, thinking about, and any emotional responses they have. Since many people find it uncomfortable to say anything negative or may forget about the think-aloud protocol, during the study the facilitator may need to encourage or remind the user.

Make the written tasks available to the user one at a time so the user can refer to the current task's instructions without being distracted by the upcoming tasks. Don't interrupt the user during the study unless it is absolutely necessary. All you need to do is to observe and take notes. You can provide clarification of the tasks if the user asks, but you should avoid suggestions about what to look at, what to think, or what to do.

There may be situations where the user is stuck, perhaps because of limitations with the prototype or because the user truly can't complete the task. In those situations you may need to prompt or help the user for the study to continue.

Quick analysis

Take a moment immediately after the session to write down the top issues you noticed or other observations you made while they are still fresh in your memory. You will immediately see trends, and often this quick list will give you a significant percentage of the major findings without spending a lot of time digging through your notes and recordings. It is especially useful when you are under time constraints or want fast design iterations.

In-depth analysis

If you have the time or desire you can also break down usability tasks into several quantitative facets. Many researchers break down test results to detail things like how many people successfully finish a certain task versus how many people failed, how many people finished the task without any problems, and how many people finished but with medium or high-level struggles. You can couple this with the feedback each user gave during the testing sessions.

Based on your intended audience, you can group and summarize major issues into areas for improvement such as "navigation problems" or "confusing terminology".

Usability data & design

For UX Designers, the ultimate goal of doing usability testing is to improve the product or design based. While usability testing can reveal areas where users had problems, it can't tell the designer what to do about them. As a designer you must rely on analysis, creativity, and judgement to transform the testing results into better designs.

It takes practice to become proficient in the art of usability data interpretation. Often what is described as a specific "usability issue" is different than the root problem, and sometimes simply addressing the usability issue on its own may not solve the larger problem.

For example, the usability test data might say the users couldn't complete a task because there were confused by a specific button's label. To some people this would suggest that the user could complete the task if the button had a better label. However, the real problem might be that the page flow relies on what might be an unnecessary action triggered by that button. Instead of renaming the button it might be better to redesign the page flow in a way that doesn't require the action, eliminating the need for the button and removing a step for the user.

5
UX Design
Competency

"A designer is an emerging synthesis of artist, inventor, mechanic, objective economist and evolutionary strategist."

R. Buckminster Fuller

The previous chapters give a sense of the overall UX Design process, along with the common methods and tools that should be part of your "design tool belt". It is possible that you are already very fluent in many of them. However, UX Design competency is much more than just knowledge of tools, methods, and processes. There is a vast collection of abilities, knowledge, and skills that make up UX Design competency. This chapter discusses them and provide suggestions for how you can get better at them.

Don't worry about trying to master everything that is described in this chapter. You don't need to be an expert at every single aspect mentioned below to be a great designer. Very few designers are fluent in all of these areas, and those that are have only become that way after many, many years of practice. Secondly, you are surely already good at some of them. Self-assess what you already know and lean on the strengths you have. With the advice in this chapter you can identify gaps in your expertise to formulate a plan for improvement.

We break UX Design competency up into 4 different areas:

Cognitive Abilities
Your ability to empathize, interpret, analyze, and imagine.

Knowledge
Familiarity with many different fields in addition to design.

Design Judgement
Your ability to draw conclusions and make decisions regarding UX Design practice, cultivated through experience.

Soft Skills
Your ability to communicate, collaborate, lead, learn, and critique.

Cognitive Abilities

Cognitive abilities are the kinds of abilities that everyone has in some measure. These abilities can be built like muscles, but the brain needs to use them often in order to get better.

Empathy

Empathy is your capacity to be aware of, understand, and to vicariously experience the emotions, feelings, attitudes, and thoughts of another person. All UX Designers must have empathy. It allows you to put yourself into someone else's situation and come up with solutions that serve them instead of yourself.

Good designers know that empathy isn't something that you can acquire just by looking at user data, as it is much more than just being able to describe or have knowledge of someone else's situation. It is a complex notion that is rooted in genuine respect and a desire to care for others. True empathy is something you feel in addition to something you think.

{ "Empathy is about finding echoes of another person in yourself."

- Mohsin Hamid }

Although empathy is an innate quality shared by all people, for various reasons some people have a lesser or stronger capacity for it. Luckily it can be cultivated through practice, experience, and exposure to the people you are designing for.

Interpretation and Analysis

Interpretation and analysis are cognitive skills constantly used by UX Designers. You will need these skills to interpret the design problem and derive insights from user research data, to critique your own designs to improve upon them, to learn from the work of others, and to effectively collaborate with others. Like other cognitive abilities, we all have them but you must practice and reflect to improve upon them.

Imagination

> "Without leaps of imagination or dreaming, we lose the excitement of possibilities. Dreaming, after all is a form of planning."
>
> - Gloria Steinem

As a creative profession imagination is core to what we do. Without imagination there is no design because design involves coming up with things that never existed before. At some point in the past there was a UI need for a user to select an option from a list of options without showing all of them on the screen at once, but a "dropdown list" UI element didn't exist. Someone had to imagine it.

As with all other cognitive abilities, imagination is something we all have as human beings. While some people seem to be more imaginative than others, the creative part of the brain is like a muscle. The more you use it the stronger it becomes, and you will find that imagination and creation come more naturally. To practice this you should not limit yourself to UX Design activities. You can make hand crafts, work on a do-it-yourself project, compose a song, write a play, make a video, or draw comics. Do whatever suits you. Better yet, pick something that doesn't suit you and see what you learn from it.

Knowledge

While cognitive abilities require your brain to be highly engaged and are maintained through practice, knowledge is simply information you internalize and call to memory as needed. Knowledge is gained through accumulation via practice and exposure. UX Design competency requires knowledge in a wide range of topics.

Design Principles

Design principles are general rules or best design practices. There are generic universal design principles that are applicable to many design domains, and specific ones such as visual design principles, mobile design principles, web design principles, and so on. Every method or practice has a set of summarized principles that have been distilled over time to guide future practice. Many company design teams have their own set of design principles created specifically for that company's products.

The best way to acquire knowledge of design principles is by accumulation. A great place to start is with Lidwell, Holden, and Butler's Universal Principles of Design. And as always, there is no substitute for practice.

UI patterns

UI patterns refer to recurring solutions for common UI design problems. For example, a dropdown list menu is a common UI pattern for only allowing the selection of one item out of many items, given a limited space. Familiarity with common UI patterns will save you a lot of time so that you don't spend time "reinventing the wheel", and you can focus on solving larger UX problems. It also improves the usability of your design because people are already familiar with how most common UI patterns work.

There are plenty of resources available for learning UI patterns. Many companies establish their own pattern libraries as a way to document internal UI knowledge as well as ensure consistency across their products. Some companies even make them publicly available, such as MailChimp, Yahoo, and Android Developers. There are also inspirational libraries such as PatternTap, which collects and organizes real world uses of UI patterns with references to the original source. We have listed a variety of online UI pattern resources in Chapter 7.

Visual Design

Even though UX Design and Visual design are often considered separate job functions, as a UX Designer you need to have a good sense of visual design and at least some basic production skills. Visual design is not separable from the overall user experience, and you will need some visual design abilities to understand how content will look on a page and what constitutes an effective UI layout and hierarchy. To work effectively with with visual designers you must be able to communicate the visual goals of the design, what emotions to evoke, and how the visual design will affect the overall experience.

UX Designers also need visual design skills to create effective design deliverables. Persona documents, wireframes, prototypes, specifications, and presentations are all visual artifacts. You must have some visual production skills to make your design deliverables more professional and effective.

Front-end development

All parts of software development influence the user's experience, but the front-end UI is what the user directly interacts with. You need to have at least a basic knowledge of front-end development so you can better understand the constraints of the medium, which will help you to be creative within the limits of what is feasible. It will also help you to collaborate and communicate with front-end developers.

A working knowledge of front-end development also enables you to produce high-fidelity prototypes. For beginners we recommend starting with web development since it is easier to learn compared to other platforms, and a huge portion of modern digital products involve web applications. There are number of online resources, books, or college courses to help you learn. Codecademy is a great online resource with highly effective course material. You can also learn by creating a web-based design portfolio.

As for mobile applications, web knowledge will only get you so far. You also need to be familiar with mobile-specific knowledge such as device sizes and how touch interactions are different from keyboard and mouse input. The mobile UI field is changing quickly, and UX Designers have to keep up with the latest developments and trends.

Technology

UX Designers work on digital products, so in addition to common digital technology knowledge such as web and mobile, you will also need to gain domain-specific technology knowledge. For example, if you are designing a tool for digital advertisers then you will need to understand how digital ads are produced, stored, and served as well as how ad networks and ad exchanges work. If you are designing an application for data storage administrators you will need to know how data is stored, backed up, and organized as well as how networks, hard drives, and servers work.

You do not need to take classes or read a dozen books on every technology domain. Most domain knowledge is learned on the job. Many companies provide a plethora of training materials when you are hired, but they aren't always enough. UX Designers should also listen carefully during meetings when the conversation moves into technical topics (sometimes this is not an easy thing to do). If you don't understand, ask lots of questions about how things work. Developers and engineers are usually happy to give you a primer or learning session. Not only does this help you understand and design better, but it also fosters good relationships and a collaborative culture.

Psychology and Cognitive Science

To effectively design for people's needs you must have knowledge of how people perceive the world around them, how they think, what motivates them, and how they make decisions. Any additional background or education you can get in psychology and cognitive science will make you a much better designer. For a good idea of how psychology and cognitive science are incorporated into design, we recommend reading <u>100 Things Every Designer Should Know About People</u> by Susan Weinschenk.

Product Management & Business

In many places the field of UX Design is becoming understood inherently as the digital equivalent of Product Design. This means that a UX Designer's job is not just to represent the user, but also to create products that provide business value in doing so.

UX Designers need to have at least a basic understanding of product management, business, and marketing to situate UX work into the larger company goals. The ability to speak the language of product management, business, and marketing will make you a trusted partner in the decision-making process. You will know how to avoid wasting effort if you understand the actual business costs associated with particular product design decisions or changes.

One of the most effective and inexpensive ways to learn about product management and business is simply to pay attention to more than the design side of things at your job. Pay attention to how product managers think and talk. Ask questions about how they make decisions and how your role as a designer can help them. Just like every other stakeholder, most product managers, business analysts, and marketers are more than willing to explain their role.

Content Strategy and Copy Writing

Content, meaning the text used in the interface, website, or printed material, is a crucial part of the design. Even though most companies have copy writers and content strategists, as a UX Designer you must be able to write good content. UX Designers must communicate effectively, and writing is a fundamental method of communication. You can't be a good designer if you can't wield words effectively.

This doesn't mean you have to be a master linguist or author, but you do need to have good judgement about how words affect the user experience. Words have connotations that convey voice or tone that should be accounted for in the UX Design process. For example, the word "submit" is a common action label for a button that sends user input into a system, but it sometimes has a slightly negative or sterile connotation. Perhaps your particular design situation calls for a more specific, slightly positive action like "send".

You may also need to plan for localization if your product will be available in multiple languages. For example, English words can be up to 3 times longer when translated to German. This has a significant impact on how you organize the interface.

Design Judgement

Design judgement is often considered to be an abstract and loaded term. Some people consider judgement to be no different than opinion, but for a designer judgement is something you rely on for everything you do. When we say judgement we mean your ability to draw conclusions and make decisions regarding UX Design practice. There is never enough data to tell you exactly what to do in a given situation. A designer's judgement is what helps them make decisions. This is especially true in when there is no clear path forward.

Design can be unpredictable and messy. It is fair to say that design judgement is the one thing that lets you navigate and adapt regardless of the situation. Should you conduct interviews or use a focus group? Should you combine two similar personas into a single persona? Should you spend your time learning more about the domain or sketching another design concept? Do you need another round of usability testing? How should you structure your presentation so that it is easier for everyone to understand the design rationale? Is this design good? Is this design good *enough*?

Judgement is not a scientific, logical skill set but it is indeed a real, tangible, valuable thing. It is a unique personal blend of your own experience, thoughts, and philosophies. The best advice we can give to cultivate your own design judgement is to practice, be patient, and most importantly reflect upon your work.

Soft Skills

Design doesn't happen in vacuum. UX Designers are constantly working with other people, requiring soft skills to effectively work with stakeholders and see projects through from beginning to end.

Communication and presentation

Design solutions must be communicated to be understood. UX Designers often provide a stream of insights, goals, concepts, changes, and other aspects of design in order to make projects proceed smoothly. Designers have to wield visual, verbal, and written forms of communication appropriately to communicate effectively.

One of the most important, complex, and common forms of communication for UX Design is presentation. If you are working in-house you will need to present design at different stages to align cross-functional teams and to get feedback, budget, support, and sign-off. If you are at a design agency you will need to present the design to your client at different stages to get buy-in. Some people find it difficult to craft a good presentation, but UX Designers should be natural storytellers. The main way to get better is with deliberate practice, but here are some good tips for your next presentation:

> - Set the stage.
> - Tell a story.
> - Know your audience and presentation goals.
> - Craft good content.

Set the stage.

Don't jump to the design solutions right away. Start with a clear statement about the problem(s) you are solving, who the users are, and what they are like. List any relevant assumptions, design goals and principles, insights, and scope. This paints the target of what your design is aiming at along with the context around it. Also, make sure to describe the process you are using and what stage you are at.

Tell a story.

Slideshows with just a series of screens or facts and figures are not engaging. You have to tell a story with your screens, and put the use of your design solution in a scenario. This way people see not only what the design is but also how it is used. If you have storyboards as part of your design process now is a great time to use them.

Know your audience and presentation goals.

Treat your presentation just like any other design challenge. You have a user base (the audience) and a goal, which may be to gather feedback, align strategies, or get buy-in on a design concept. Your presentation style and content should reflect the needs of the audience and the goals of the presentation.

Is it an informal presentation to the product manager just to get his feedback and brainstorm with you? Is it a formal presentation to the VP of Product Development with all the product managers and development managers to align cross-product UX strategies? Or is it a design critique session with your fellow designers? Are the audience members hearing about this design for the first time?

Craft good content.

We have all seen presentations where someone "presents" by reading bullet points and text from a PowerPoint slide. Designers should never be so bland. Your audience will be bored, disengaged, and untrusting of your design solution.

When you present your design, be creative with the medium. Provide physical materials. Make a video. Act out a scene if that it is the best way to engage the audience and get your point across. Remember that people should be paying attention to you and the design. Your presentation will suffer if the audience is reading words from a screen or thinking about the decorative PowerPoint template you chose instead of listening to you.

If you use a slideshow application, put your UI and visual design skills to work! Here's a few handy tips for making your slideshow:

- Don't rely on generic, default themes.
- Minimize the amount of words on each slide.
- Focus on images and storytelling.
- Use transitions sparingly.

Don't rely on the themes provided by Powerpoint or Keynote.
Instead, create your own style that is appropriate for your audience. If you aren't confident in your visual design skills an easy and effective approach is just plain white or black slides.

Minimize the amount of words on each slide.
If your audience is reading they aren't listening to you. Also, when you use less words the words you do include will be more powerful.

Focus on images and storytelling.
Use your storyboards and incorporate your UI into the flow of the story.

Use transitions sparingly.
Transitions are distracting. Don't use a transition unless it actually enhances the presentation in some way.

Collaboration

UX Design is a highly collaborative job, especially if you are working at a company. You will likely always be part of a larger product team, potentially working with many different job functions on a day-to-day basis. The key to being a good collaborator is to be a willing listener. The same empathy that helps you to understand and design for your users will help you when collaborating with other people in the design process. You must genuinely attempt to hear what others say without feeling like your ideas need to be heard above others' ideas.

Facilitation and Leadership

"The way a team plays as a whole determines its success. You may have the greatest bunch of individual stars in the world, but if they don't play together, the club won't be worth a dime."

- Babe Ruth

If you have ever participated in a group project you know that a well-facilitated and organized group produces the best results. For the best possible design outcome all affecting factors need to work in sync, which takes a great deal of leadership and facilitation skills. As you grow in your career you may choose to take on a more senior leadership role where you will spend more time leading and facilitating and less time on the detailed design work itself.

Primary and Lead UX Designers are typically responsible for organizing and leading the design effort. This means organizing and facilitating meetings to discuss design goals, align design visions, brainstorm solutions, and critique design. The lead designer will work with the researcher to figure out the research plan and timeline. The lead designer also needs to bring in the prototyper and visual designer at the right time so that nothing is being bottlenecked.

The lead designer also decides when and how to review design with cross-functional teams and facilitate the discussion so that meetings stay on topic and the feedback is timely and actionable.

Fast Learning

While Chapter 3 is dedicated to advice to learn UX Design, you must also be able to quickly grasp new concepts and knowledge from outside the realm of design. Every project will require you to learn something new.

This is true no matter where you are, but is especially the case if you are at an agency. One month you may need to quickly understand dividends, IRAs, and bonds to work on a personal finance tool and the next month become fluent in what types of makeup are best for different skin types so you can design a shopping experience for a cosmetics app. Even if you are working as an in-house designer and have the benefit of staying in the same domain, you will still need to grasp a lot of domain knowledge over time to really excel at your job.

The following is a list of behaviors common to people who are able to learn quickly:

- Make learning a habit.
- Read.
- Find knowledgeable people and ask them questions.
- Find opportunities to teach.
- Don't ignore things you don't understand.

Make learning a habit.

"Learning never exhausts the mind."

- Leonardo da Vinci

Push yourself to learn new things. It doesn't matter if you choose to study a different language, take a crafting class, or pick up production design skills from watching videos online. All that matters is that you make it a habit.

Read.

There is no better way to expose yourself to new ideas and inspiration than through reading. And as one of our trusted design colleagues likes to say, don't just read "fast-food" design blogs and easily consumable UX advice. Those may be great for daily readings or staying up to date on industry trends, but make sure to mix in something heady and complex to round out your growth. We have included a list of recommended reading materials in Chapter 7.

Find knowledgeable people and ask them questions.

If someone is willing to be your mentor, even better.

Find opportunities to teach.

You learn things much more deeply when you are forced to summarize and explain the topic in ways that resonate with others.

Don't ignore things you don't understand.

Pretty much the entire collection of human knowledge is available through an Internet connection. If you encounter a concept, phrase, word, or topic that you aren't familiar with, look it up. It often doesn't take long, and it will provide you with the context or history that your brain needs to form connections and commit the knowledge to permanent memory.

Design Critique

You will often be asked to provide your professional thoughts and judgement of other people's work in formal or informal settings. This is called design critique, and it is vital to good UX Design work. Good

UX Design critique helps other people improve their work and establishes your expertise, professionalism, and authority.

There are two elements to giving good design critique: the insights you have and the way in which you deliver those insights. You can use any design around you to practice the first. Think about an app on your phone and ask yourself where it could be improved. What would you improve first? Can you infer any assumptions the app makes about the users? What were the design's goals? What were the business's goals? Did the design achieve them?

It is also important to think about what the design does well. Design critique isn't just about finding problems, but is also about identifying and celebrating what works well. If you practice this regularly you will become more and more insightful about design and accumulate design inspiration and patterns for use in your own work.

As for how to deliver your design critique to others, think about how you prefer to receive critique. It is often a good technique to make positive comments first before moving to areas of improvement. Provide rationale for your feedback and tie your reasoning to the design goals, the problem, and the users.

It is very important to avoid speaking in terms of your personal preference such as, "I don't like tabs as a navigation pattern." Instead you should describe why it might not work for this design. It would be better to say, "Using tabs here for navigation is not appropriate because the user has to switch between the tabs to get to vital and related information."

Be conscious of your audience and what type of feedback is being solicited. If another designer has asked for feedback on the navigation, make sure to provide feedback on the navigation before pointing out that the icons in the footer are confusing.

The way you conduct yourself when you receive critique is just as important as how you give it. UX Designers are constantly showing their work, and everyone who sees it will have an opinion about it. Most of them won't be designers, and many of them won't abide by the advice we provided about how to give good critique. This is just the nature of doing design work. You must be open to critique from all types of people and develop a professional way to respond. Each personality handles this differently, but here are a few tips for handling critique in a professional manner:

- Let the audience know what kind of feedback you want.
- Don't get defensive.
- Be open.

Let the audience know what kind of feedback you want.

People with a vested interest in the design will have a lot to say, but a very good technique is to create feedback rules for your meeting, team, or product organization. Our good friend (and design mentor) Matt Snyder likes to use the 30% rule, which is to require that the audience voice only the most important 30% of their feedback.

Also, don't be surprised if people deviate from what you ask them to focus on. Politely thank them for their feedback and ask if they have any feedback on the elements you need input on.

Don't get defensive.

If someone says something you don't agree with, make a note of it and thank the person for their feedback. Design critiques are typically a time for collecting feedback, not for defending every decision that was made. As a designer it is up to your judgement if you want to alter the design based on the feedback you get.

Be open.

This is especially important when you hear something you don't agree with. Later on when you look at your notes, give the feedback at least a moment of honest consideration. Sometimes your initial instincts are right and the feedback won't help you push the design forward. However, you will be surprised at how often the feedback you initially wanted to dismiss ends up being what sparks your next good idea.

As we have mentioned many times already, all these skills come with practice. Luckily you more or less already have some of these skills. Many of the skills listed here are not like sewing skills in that if you have never done it before you have to start from nothing. You have surely already worked in teams, interviewed people, practiced your communication skills, and been in situations where you had to learn all kinds of new things.

So don't feel discouraged if it seems like there is a lot to learn. This chapter described a wide array of skills needed by UX Designers, but as we said you have many of them already. All you need to do is be aware of them so you can get better through practice and reflection.

6
Jobs

"Searching for a job is like a piñata. If you hit it hard enough you will be rewarded."

Terry Hall

The job market for UX Design has never been hotter than it is right now, and it doesn't seem like it will slow down any time in the near future. In addition to the typical software company and design agency positions, nearly every industry and domain is looking for UX Design talent. Any company looking to improve their products and services wants design help including medical device manufacturers, insurance companies, universities, and everything in-between.

However, even though there are lots of opportunities out there it can be fairly difficult to land your first UX Design position. This goal of this chapter is to arm you with the knowledge you need to find a UX Design position by detailing what kinds of jobs there are, how to prepare your application package, find UX Design positions, and what to expect during the interview process.

There are mainly four types of UX Design jobs, each with its own pros and cons: in-house, consultancy, contractor, and freelance. Most designers who are just starting out focus on in-house design positions, so the advice in this chapter regarding finding and applying to jobs is focused on in-house jobs. However, it is very common for designers to try multiple job types in their career.

UX Design Job Types

In-house

An in-house UX Design position is when you are an employee of a company and UX Design is a job function within the company. In-house designers are often assigned to one or two products and work on them for over a long period of time. They are part of the cross-functional product team and often work closely together with product managers and developers. Most of the time in-house designers belong to the UX team and report to UX managers or directors.

Pros:

In-house UX Designers tend to feel more ownership of the products they work on. It is rewarding to see a product evolve over time, and you get the chance to correct mistakes or improve in future releases. The salary and benefits for in-house designers are often much higher than other types of jobs.

Cons:

As an in-house designer you tend to get less exposure to different types of projects and domains. If you are an in-house designer at a finance-related company, your design skill set will be focused on finance. This is great if you are interested in finance but if you want broader experience you likely won't get it. This is one reason many UX Designers average about 1-2 years at in-house jobs before they end up looking for other opportunities.

Also, if the company is still trying to figure out how to fit UX Design into their processes the design environment might not be the best for you to produce good work. It is possible that you could face an uphill battle as the organization struggles to evolve, and there can be conflicts and confusion regarding philosophy, approach, methods, and even job roles.

Corporations vs. Startups

Corporations typically have been around longer than startups and have an established product lifecycle and slow pace of change. Corporations typically have more budget than startups, so the UX team is likely to have more people you can learn from. It is possible that the UX team might be more established, so you can rely on past work of the designers to ease the transition.

With UX Design being introduced to corporations as a relatively new job function, it is likely to take a long time to fully become part of the product development process. The UX team is likely to spend a lot of time figuring out how to incorporate their processes, philosophies, and approaches into the existing environment. There can be friction with cross-functional teams, and even political power struggles.

On the other hand, startups are younger and more likely to understand the importance of UX Design from the inception. This doesn't mean that they have perfect UX Design processes, but since they are nimble and fast-paced they mature faster. UX teams are often not established at startups, so you might be the only one if the company is still very small. In those situations you probably will wear multiple hats, serving as a researcher, interaction designer, visual designer, prototyper, or even UI developer.

At a startup you may be able to influence and shape the product development process more easily than in a big company, as there is less red tape. However, the environment is much less stable. Product direction, process, organizational structure, job security, budget, and even where your desk is located could all be in flux.

Enterprise vs. Consumer

Regardless of whether you work in a large corporation or at a startup, you will either be working on enterprise products or consumer products. Enterprise products are mainly used by companies, such as tools for monitoring web security across a company intranet or managing inventory at a warehouse. Consumer products are for the general public, such as TurboTax personal finance software or the FitBit personal fitness products. There are of course products that serve both consumer and enterprise customers such as SurveyMonkey, Gmail, and Dropbox.

Enterprise product design often requires a lot of domain knowledge, making the ramp up time longer than designing for consumer products. In consumer products UX Design has a clear impact on company profits, while in enterprise software UX's contribution to the bottom line is likely to be vague and indirect.

Enterprise products have a much higher tolerance for poor customer experience and usability due to the complexity and age of the products and the fact that most revenue models are contract-based. Enterprise software contracts are based on fulfilling feature requirements, so product development still tends to focus on features and capabilities ahead of improved usability.

To be clear we are not implying that enterprise product design should be avoided, but it is important to understand the realities before deciding to take an enterprise software job.

Design Consultancies and Agencies

UX Design jobs can also be found at consulting firms and agencies. In an agency you are typically assigned to a client for the duration of a project. The work will vary a lot depending on the project and the type of agency you work for. After the contractual obligations have been met on the project, you will move on to the next project.

Pros:
You are likely to work with like-minded people who speak the same design language. You can be exposed to many different projects in a short amount of time, and you can build up design experience in many domains. You can grow very quickly with the right guidance from senior members in the firm, not just in design skills but also soft skills such as the ability to communicate, present, and sell design.

Cons:
Consultancy jobs can be very demanding. You may need to regularly put in more hours than you would at other jobs. The salary is typically lower than in-house design jobs, with less enticing benefits packages.

Contractor

There are also contracting positions at both companies and agencies, typically ranging from a couple of months up to a year. Contracting positions can be temporary, or are sometimes contract-to-hire positions where the intention is to eventually convert you to a full-time employee. You can either look for and apply to contracting positions yourself or work with a contracting or recruiting firm.

Pros:

You stand a better chance of working on a good range of projects depending on what contracting positions you get. You get to control your own work fate because when the contract is ended you have no obligation to continue with the job. Also, due to the lack of benefits you can typically negotiate a much higher hourly pay rate than any other design job.

Cons:

Your income might not be stable if you rely on short-term contracts, and you may have to spend a lot of effort to secure your next contract before your current contract ends. Contractors rarely receive any job benefits, meaning you will have to handle medical, dental, and other insurance costs on your own.

Freelancing or Starting Your Own Consultancy

You can also work as a freelancer or operate as your own design consultancy. You take on client projects yourself and hire others or subcontract as needed. Freelancers often utilize a hybrid model of contracting and consulting, especially when they first venture out on their own since they might not yet have a steady client stream.

Freelancing is not recommended for beginners. People who do this typically have lots of experience and industry connections that make it easier to secure client work.

Pros:

As a freelancer you are essentially running your own business. You get to control your work-life balance so you don't have to worry about your hours, vacation days, or sick days. Many people find it liberating not having to answer to a manager. (You do have to answer to your clients, though!)

You also get to pick your own projects and clients. If you are established or have expertise in an area you can potentially have a higher salary than if you work for someone else.

Cons:

It is hard to get started and establish a consistent stream of projects. Even at the best of times with an established brand and client network your income may not be stable. You have to manage all the aspects of your business, so you will be responsible for securing client work, bookkeeping, and marketing. You also may be subjected to more taxes and you are responsible for your own insurance costs.

Applying to a UX Job

If you don't have any experience it can be somewhat difficult to land your first UX job. That is why the advice here is focused on in-house positions, which are usually easier to get if you are just starting out. (If you are interested in agency work, much of the same advice applies.) In this section we describe how to prepare for, find, and apply to jobs, and what to expect during a typical hiring process.

Put together your application package

The very first thing you need to do is put together your application package. At a minimum you need a résumé and online portfolio, but you should also consider creating an offline version of your portfolio, a LinkedIn profile, cover letter, and maybe even a blog. Everything in this package will likely be seen by the hiring manager. Taken as a whole this package conveys your qualifications, mindset, knowledge set, skill set, and tool set to the hiring manager. Here are some tips to prepare your package:

- Be deliberate about your own brand.
- Show your process through artifacts.
- Unglamorous design experience is better than nothing.
- Visual design matters.
- Don't overdo your portfolio.

Be deliberate about your own design brand.

Your portfolio, LinkedIn profile, and résumé should tell a consistent story about your background, skill set, and who you are as a designer.

Show your process through artifacts.

When looking for UX Designers hiring managers care about your process and how you solve problems more than the final outcome. Take pictures or videos of your process including research, usability, sketches, and prototypes. If you don't have design artifacts for your projects you should generate or recreate them. All these materials reveal the design process and not just the final UI.

Unglamorous design experience is better than nothing.

If you feel like you don't have enough design projects, then do some. Volunteer to design something for someone you know or create a redesign of an existing product. It might not be an amazing portfolio, but it is better than nothing. Such a portfolio isn't going to get you a senior role at a top company, but it will certainly help you land that first internship or junior role that you need to get started.

Visual design matters.

Even if you aren't applying to a visual or graphic design position, you are still a designer and will be expected to have a good visual sense. You don't have to impress anyone with your visual design skills but you should at least choose good typography and layout for your résumé and have good pictures on your portfolio. Feel free to use a theme or template if you think it will make a better impression.

Don't overdo your portfolio.

You do not need to write every detail about every project you have ever done. You should choose your best or most representative work, and describe enough for the viewer to understand what the project was about and what you contributed. Succinctly summarize the problem or challenge, illustrate how you approached it, note key insights, and show the solution.

The hiring manager and other evaluators are not going to read every project in-depth, at least not on their first pass. They will typically skim through your portfolio as the first step to gauge if you have the design skills they need, and then decide whether to move forward with you or not. That being said, it is wise to have one or two in-depth project descriptions readily available on your site or upon request. You can even use those projects as examples during the interview process.

When it comes to your online portfolio you have plenty of options. You can create your own website, use a portfolio-centric Wordpress theme, or put your work on design portfolio sites like Behance or Coroflot. There are pros and cons of each format, and there isn't really a preferred method so just choose whichever you are comfortable with. (Some designers choose to use them all.)

Keep in mind that the design of your portfolio will affect the hiring manager's perception of you as a UX Designer. If your own site is hard to navigate or the content is hard to follow, it won't give them confidence that you will design good experiences for their products.

Use lots of images to show whatever is relevant from the process: prototypes, testing sessions, wireframes, and storyboards. Of course, if there is a final product you should include it in your site or link to it. It is also good practice to keep an offline version of your portfolio in PDF form so it is easy to email, print, or present on short notice.

Finding and applying to job openings

Once you have put together your application package you should be ready to look for and apply to job openings. There are three main ways to find job openings: job boards, recruiters, and networking. You will likely need to use all three to find your first job. Personally, we have continued to use all three throughout our careers.

Job Boards

The most common way to start looking for UX Design jobs is through job posting sites like Indeed, Monster, and LinkedIn. There are even job posting accounts on social media, such as @UXJobs on Twitter. If there is a particular company you want to work for, you can search for jobs on their website. If you are just starting out you probably want to focus on junior level jobs and intern positions that don't require many years of experience.

While there are plenty of UX jobs out there, it can be difficult to know what fits you because UX Design positions are called many different things in the industry. You should be flexible in your search and use multiple titles such as UX Designer, UI Designer, Interaction Designer, Product Designer, User Researcher, or even Usability Engineer. You can't assume what the job requires based solely on the title, so make sure to read the requirements in the job posting.

Recruiters

Scouring job boards isn't the only way to find a job in UX Design. There are large and small recruiting firms that place people at jobs, with some focused solely on UX or related design jobs. You don't have to pay anything since the recruiter gets a commission from the company if and when you accept the job offer. Recruiters typically (but not always) look for candidates with some kind of job experience. Bear this in mind if you are a new graduate, as you may want to focus your efforts on networking or using the career services department at your school.

Recruiters have a wide network of companies they work with to find qualified candidates. They are often well-versed at the job type (in our case UX), the market, and the talent needed for the job. Some recruiters even negotiate offers for you if their commission is based on a percentage of your salary. In addition to helping place candidates at jobs, recruiters also host local networking events so that you can talk to multiple companies in a relatively short amount of time.

If you choose to work with a recruiter make sure you communicate clearly what type of job you want (contractor or full-time), your qualifications, and motivations. The more they know about you the better match they can provide. Of course each recruiter's expertise will vary, even within the same firm, and keep in mind that even if you work with the best recruiter it is still not guaranteed that they will find a position for you. You can also work with multiple recruiters and firms at the same time as there are no obligations on your side.

Networking

It is common knowledge that networking is important for any job hunt, and this is especially true when you are just starting out. In most companies internal referrals are given the highest priority. The referral won't guarantee a job but often you will at least get a phone interview. If you don't have a job now, let the whole world know you are looking for one through social media and reach out to your key connections individually. (But if you are currently employed you need to exercise more discretion!)

UX Design is a very welcoming and close-knit community so it is relatively easy to build your network. LinkedIn (in addition to many other online networking sites) is a great tool to build your network and let people know you are looking for a job. You should also attend UX Design talks and networking events in your area to forge face-to-face relationships. If there aren't any UX meetups in your area, feel free to organize one yourself. It's a good bet that plenty of people near you would love to meet and share knowledge if you provide the venue.

The Hiring Panel and Process

Your application package, connections, and recruiters can get you the first interview but it is up to you to get the job. The hiring process is different for different companies, but we have tried to break it down into the typical elements that apply to most situations. In general the process typically involves talking with different members of a hiring panel, going to an onsite interview, and completing a design task of some sort.

Hiring Panel

The hiring panel is the group of stakeholders involved with hiring you. Some companies have dozens of people on the hiring panel and some have just one or two who will fulfill multiple roles. The following is a list of the people you will typically encounter on the hiring panel during the interview process.

In-house Recruiter

Many companies have in-house recruiters who are responsible for finding and screening potential candidates. This person is different than the third-party recruiter previously mentioned in this chapter, but they fill similar roles. The in-house recruiter will be your point of contact and will schedule interviews, pass along your résumé and portfolio, and handle your paperwork.

Hiring Manager
The hiring manager is the final decision maker on whether or not you are offered the job. This person is typically the UX Manager or Director, but may have a variety of other titles depending on what department UX Design is in. If the hiring manager is a non-UX Design role, make sure to ask questions about the nature of UX Design in that organization.

UX Interviewers
Some or all of the members of the UX team are very likely to be part of the interview panel. They evaluate you based on their judgement and job function. For example, during the interview the graphic designer will want to know how you would involve them in your design process, evaluating what it will be like to collaborate with you. The various UX interviewers give their assessments of you to the hiring manager and make their individual hiring recommendations.

Cross-functional Team Interviewers
There will be representatives from other job functions on the panel as well. The most common cross-functional team representatives are product managers and developers. They are there mainly to evaluate how well you understand the overall product development process and what it will be like to collaborate with you.

The Hiring Process
Now that you know the members of the hiring panel, we will take a look at the common steps of the hiring process and how you can prepare for each one. Keep in mind that the hiring process is just as much about you deciding if you want to work for the company as

much as it is about the company deciding to hire you. Use the process to get a feel for the company and what your job will be like.

Recruiter Screening

Whether you are working with third-party recruiters or an in-house recruiter, you will participate in some kind of initial screening. The recruiter might have gotten your name from a contact or they may have pulled your application out of their database and decided to give you a call. This is typically a short phone call or email discussion to establish contact with you, make sure you are interested in the position, and get some basic information about you. Some recruiters might ask questions related to design or ask about your design background and experience.

The purpose of this screening is to see if you fit what this position is looking for. The conversation is typically very casual without a lot of pressure or expectations by either party, so you don't need to prepare anything. You might bypass this step if you have an internal referral.

Phone Interview

After the recruiter screening you are likely to get one or more phone interviews, typically with the hiring manager or other UX team members. The recruiter will let you know the time, length, and who you will be talking to ahead of time. The topic of these phone interviews will mostly be about your design skills, background, and ability to communicate. It is important to be well-prepared.

The first thing to do when preparing for the phone interview is to look up information about the people you will be talking to. LinkedIn is a good place to find out their educational and work background. Check out their portfolio or blog to find out what they are like as UX professionals. Do you share the same philosophy? Do you like their work? Did you go to the same school? All of the information will help you get to know this person before talking to him or her.

You may feel apprehensive about researching your interviewers, but you shouldn't. Believe us, they are most definitely researching you. As long as your research is professional in nature your interviewers will just feel that you are taking the opportunity seriously. Use this information to prepare, but don't try to cater your answer to their liking based on your assumptions. You will come across as disingenuous and good interviewers will see right through it.

Secondly, it is helpful to prepare talking points. Here are some typical questions you will be asked early in the hiring process so make sure you are prepared to respond to them:

- How and why did you get into the field of UX Design?

- What is your design philosophy?

- What is a product you think has good user experience and why do you think it is good?

- How do you keep up to date on the UX Design field?

It is also possible they will want to discuss a project in your portfolio in detail. You should be familiar with the projects in your portfolio, so review them again if you need to refresh your memory. Be prepared to walk someone through the project, conveying your design thinking and expertise without boring them. It is a good idea to write down key points on index cards or Post-it notes and have them in front of you during the phone call.

The last few minutes of the phone call will be reserved for you to ask questions. Prepare a few questions ahead of time since you only have a few minutes. Ask whatever is most important for you to determine if the job is right for you. You might want to ask about the team structure, how UX Design fits into the product development process, or details on work benefits.

Design Homework

Some companies require design candidates to complete a small design project, but not always. The design project format varies from half-hour onsite exercises to 48-hour design challenges which you may be asked to do before coming onsite. What they all have in common is that the hiring panel is looking for how you think about, approach, and solve problems. In most cases the design solution itself doesn't matter that much. A great design solution will certainly impress, but it is more important to clearly communicate your process.

If you were given a design challenge to complete offsite make sure to organize your design assets before you send them along. (We have seen some candidates just dump a bunch of documents in a folder and send it all back. Trust us, those candidates did not receive job offers.)

Make sure you provide design assets that can be understood without you there to explain them. Create a presentation or design document that includes any research you did, personas you used, similar designs you evaluated, any prototyping and validation you did, and what you learned.

Onsite Interview

The onsite interview is typically the last step in the interview process. You are likely to spend half a day to a full day interviewing with the hiring panel. The onsite interview usually involves a variety of sessions including a presentation (by you), mini design tasks, and one-on-one interviews with various team members.

> "A good portfolio will get you an interview. A good attitude will get you a job."
>
> - Marty Amsler

At this stage the hiring team may already have a pretty good idea of your design abilities, so in addition to design-related talking points don't be afraid of getting a little personal when introducing yourself. The hiring panel is looking for someone to join their team, which involves more than your production and problem solving skills. There needs to be some kind of chemistry for the team to know that you will fit in and collaborate effectively with them. Feel free to talk about your hobbies and interests beyond UX Design.

If you are asked to prepare something ahead of time make sure to ask for instructions regarding what they want to see. They typically want you to talk through a design project from your portfolio, or the design challenge if they required you to complete one. Sometimes they don't give any instructions at all and it will be up to you to decide what is important to present to them.

No matter the content or format of the presentation, this is a prime opportunity to show who you are and how you communicate in addition to what you can do. The most important thing for this stage is to be fully prepared. If you haven't had much experience presenting, practice ahead of time with your friends and family.

You may have heard about design interviews where the designer is asked very difficult questions and is bombarded with negative feedback. This is not the norm, but there are some interviewers who will do this just see how you react. If you find yourself in this situation, don't panic. The worst thing you can do is to get agitated or defensive. Answer the questions professionally and calmly, and if you don't have an answer you should just say that you don't know.

During the interview it is very likely you will be asked to participate in a mini design session. This is mainly to see how well you can think on the spot. Again, the primary goal isn't to come up with good solutions but instead to come up with approaches to tackle the problem. Don't jump into solutions at the beginning. Think aloud and explain what you think of the problem, who the users might be, what they need to achieve, any insights you have from your past experience, and what assumptions might be reasonable to make.

Consider the time you have and what you need to deliver, then propose a process within that time frame. The hiring person is likely to get involved to brainstorm with you or may ask you to change directions altogether. Just go with the flow and consider it as a real working session. They will pay close attention to how you rationalize your design decisions and how you react to feedback (especially negative feedback).

You will also likely meet with team members outside the UX Design team such as product managers and developers. In these interviews they will be looking for someone who understands what they do and is easy to work with. You will be asked questions regarding tradeoffs between design and business or engineering needs. This is also a good time to ask how they work with the current design team as their answers can help you evaluate whether this environment is desirable for you or not.

On the day of your onsite interview you should have a one-on-one conversation with the hiring manager. Your discussion with the hiring manager is usually less about assessing your design abilities and more about assessing how you would fit on the team. This is also the most important time for you to inquire about the design culture at the company and what expectations there will be for the job. Think about what kind of job you would enjoy doing every day, and use your one-on-one time with the hiring manager to collect information about this job to see how well it fits your desires.

Job Offers

Whether or not you receive the job offer is highly dependent upon two things. First, did you prove that you can do the job and quickly contribute? Don't get discouraged if you are not receiving offers because you do not have the skill set or lack experience. Build up your portfolio and focus on entry level jobs and internships. You will succeed with perseverance.

Depending on the company you are applying to, even if you already work in a related field as a graphic designer or UI developer you may find it difficult to get anything but an entry-level UX job. The reality of UX Design is that skills are gained with experience. Motivated designers will quickly turn an entry level job or internship into a higher position.

The second thing that determines if you get the job offer is if you are a good fit for the team. The question of fit is very important, and most job offers will go to the candidate who is the best fit rather than the candidate who has the best skill set or experience. Skills can be taught or gained over time, but personality and chemistry are organic.

If you do receive the job offer, then congratulations! It has likely been quite a journey. You will typically receive a verbal offer first with some room to negotiate salary and benefits. Like most jobs, salary negotiation can be tricky but will go much smoother if you are well-informed. You want to find out the average market rate in your area for the same position. There are many useful online resources that can help you like Glassdoor and Indeed. You should also ask people within your network, as they can provide you with the most up-to-date and first-hand knowledge.

Choosing the Right Job

If this is your first job in the field of UX Design you should carefully consider what you know about the role and the environment before you accept the job offer. Of course, if your options are limited then it is better to get some experience rather than none. However, if you have the choice it is better if your first job gets you exposure to many parts of the UX process rather than getting stuck in a narrow role where you only produce wireframes or conduct usability tests. If your first job doesn't help you to grow as a designer then it can be harder to get your next job.

As for whether to choose a company where the UX processes are new or established, that decision is entirely up to you. Each has their own pros and cons. In companies where UX is established you may avoid the organizational growing pains involved with incorporating UX, but you also may encounter rigid processes and limited opportunities to grow. In companies where UX is new, the constant uphill battle for recognition and support may not sound appealing but it also gives you a great opportunity to lead and shape the organization.

7
Resources

"If I have seen farther than others, it is because I was standing on the shoulders of giants."

Isaac Newton

As we mentioned in the introduction, it can be difficult for aspiring UX Designers to know where to begin since much of the information about UX is broad and disorganized. As part of this book's promise to serve as both a ramp to the UX Design field as well as a go-to reference on your journey, this chapter includes a list of links and books to help you continue learning.

In this chapter we have included what is, in our judgement, a well-rounded list long and varied enough to choose from while still short enough to be manageable. Each resource includes a short summary or description to help you decide what to add to your study list. New information and resources come out every day, but the resources here should continue to be relevant for the near future.

You can also find more resources and updated information at uxlearnersguidebook.com.

UX Design Websites

The following websites cover a wide range of topics related to UX, such as research, design principles, tools and softwares, as well as domain-specific topics such as design for eCommerce, enterprise, and so on.

nngroup.com

Nielsen Norman Group has been around since the 1990's providing UX Design related training and consulting. They also conduct their own research and publish articles and reports on almost every topic of User Experience. Their reports are often supported by lots of quantitative data from industry research. You can find them in the "Articles" and "Reports" sections of the website.

boxesandarrows.com

Boxes and Arrows offers lots of practical and well-written articles contributed by its authors covering various topics such as design principles, process and methods, softwares and tools, book reviews, and so on.

usabilitygeek.com

Don't let the name fool you. Usability Geek covers many topics beyond just usability. It started as a blog of one person, but now has grown into a publishing platform for many UX-related articles written by the owner as well as many guest authors. The articles are mostly on the design side of things more than research. You can find lots of good design guidelines and principles for user interfaces, advice for designing for eCommerce, and much more.

uie.com

Similar to Nielsen Norman Group, User Interface Engineering is also a design consulting firm providing training, research, and consultancy services. They also manage and host various UX conferences, events, publications, podcasts, and webinars. You can find a tremendous amount of free and paid learning materials there for almost every aspect of UX from philosophy and mindset, team building, and practical design tips.

uxmatters.com

Compared to many other sources, the articles on UX Matters cover not only the practice of UX Design but also things like professional development, advice for independent UX consultancies, and company design culture.

uxbooth.com

UX Booth is a very well-organized, simple to navigate, and easy to read website with articles in ten major categories. Besides the common topics they have two categories worth calling out, which are Analytics and Universal Design. The former discusses using data (mostly quantitative web analytics data) to help design. The latter discusses design practices for accessibility, an often overlooked but nonetheless important aspect of UX Design.

uxmag.com

UX Magazine is another website that covers comprehensive UX-related topics. Besides articles, you can find conferences, talks, and workshops. They also have a very active job board.

ixda.org

This is the website of the Interaction Design Association, a well-known UX Design community. There is no membership fee and you can connect with lots of UX Design practitioners online and offline. You can post a discussion online, join a local IxDA group, and find lots of information regarding events and jobs. It is a great place to learn from others and offer your own thoughts in a community of professionals and students who are passionate about the same thing.

smashingmagazine.com

Smashing Magazine has tons of well-written, useful, and practical contents covering almost every aspect that relates to the user experience of web, mobile, and other digital products. It goes beyond the usual UX topics you see in other sites, offering great content for front-end coding, graphic design, and Wordpress just to name a few. They also publish books and ebooks and organize workshops. Make sure to check out their Smashing Library, which includes a list of great books covering a wide range of topics.

alistapart.com

A List Apart publishes content dedicated to the design, development, content, and business of the web. They also have the subdivision of A Book Apart, publishing books on the same topics. They host An Event Apart, a conference focused on people who make websites. An Event Apart takes places multiple times a year in different cities.

52weeksofux.com

This is a collection of well-articulated deep thoughts related to UX, product design, and business. It is a good site to balance the purely practical resources with thought-provoking articles to help you form a deeper understanding of design and your own design philosophy.

uxmyths.com

UX Myths is a collection of misconceptions regarding UX and UI Design. Each myth and the counter arguments are well-explained.

wireframes.linowski.ca

This site has resources for wireframing, prototyping, and UI design. You can find UI stencils, icon sets, reviews of tools, and discussions on many UI-related topics.

UI Patterns and Inspiration

The following sites offer collections of UI patterns and ideas. You can find various solutions for the same UI problem, and many interesting ideas for various common UI components. They are great places for UI design inspiration.

There are dozens if not hundreds of pattern sites, but we chose the following sites because they have some of the most well-curated content and they represent a broad range of pattern types.

patterntap.com

Pattern Tap is hosted and curated by Zurb, a respected product design consultancy that seeks to empower businesses and people through design. Their pattern inspiration library is kept up to date and features handy filters to find specific patterns across many device types.

pttrns.com

Pttrns is a great resources for finding some of newest and most elegant mobile design inspirations.

littlebigdetails.com

Little Big Details is one of only a handful of sites that emphasize small, detailed interaction patterns. There is a lot of craft that goes into these details, and you can find great inspiration here.

dribbble.com

Even though Dribbble is primarily a venue for visual and graphic designers to show off their work, there are plenty of UI and interaction design samples there as well. And if you want to grow your visual design skills it is a great place to see how professional visual design is crafted.

For platform-specific patterns and interface guidelines, make sure to check out each platform's official documentation. What follows is a list of some of the most UX-related official resources for Apple, Google, and Microsoft platforms:

Apple

Main resource page for designing and developing iOS/OSX apps

https://developer.apple.com/design

UI Do's and Don'ts for Apple iOS

https://developer.apple.com/design/tips/

iOS Mobile Human Interface Guidelines

https://developer.apple.com/library/ios/documentation/UserExperie
nce/Conceptual/MobileHIG/

OS X Human Interface Guidelines

https://developer.apple.com/library/mac/documentation/UserExperi
ence/Conceptual/OSXHIGuidelines/

Google Android

Google Design Resources

http://www.google.com/design/

UI Design Guidelines for Android

http://developer.android.com/design/index.html

Google Material Design

http://www.google.com/design/spec/material-
design/introduction.html

Microsoft

Design Resources for the Windows Desktop

https://msdn.microsoft.com/en-us/windows/desktop/aa511258.aspx

Design Resources for Windows

https://dev.windows.com/en-us/design

Books

There is an ocean of books about design and user experience, but where to begin? We created this recommended reading list based on our own education, experience in the field, and from teaching others about UX. This list of books is by no means comprehensive, but it represents a wide range of essentials for someone starting out, with some deeper reads on topics vital to becoming, being, and excelling as a UX Designer.

If you are looking for more book recommendations, visit **uxlearnersguidebook.com**.

No book related to design can be easily put into one specific category, as any decent design book will cover a wide range of topics. However, for convenience we placed each book into categories based on how easy they are to read, the target audience, and their overall topic of emphasis.

Foundational UX Books

These are books you should read to get the big picture of UX, its history, and how it is situated in the industry. These books are usually part of core curriculum in schools that teach UX or IxD.

The Design of Everyday Things
Donald Norman

The Elements of User Experience
Jesse James Garrett

The Inmates are Running the Asylum: Why High Tech Products Drive Us Crazy and How to Restore the Sanity
Alan Cooper

Designing Interactions
Bill Moggridge

About Face: The Essentials of Interaction Design
Alan Cooper, Robert Reimann, David Cronin, and Christopher Noessel

Design Theory, Philosophy, and Reflection

These books go deep into the core of Design and Experience, including topics such as how designers think and work, the value(s) of design, and what it means to design for "experience".

Thoughts on Interaction Design
Jon Kolko

The Design Way: Intentional Change in an Unpredictable World
Harold Nelson and Erik Stolterman

Design Thinking: Understanding How Designers Think and Work
Nigel Cross

Technology as Experience
John McCarthy and Peter Wright

The Tacit Dimension
Michael Polanyi

Practical Guides and Design Advice

These books offer very practical advice and tips that can be quickly absorbed and applied to pretty much any project. They are great to keep around as a reference for beginners and experts alike.

Don't Make Me Think: A Common Sense Approach to Web Usability
Steve Krug

100 Things Every Designer Needs to Know About People
Susan Weinschenk

Universal Principles of Design: 125 Ways to Enhance Usability, Influence Perception, Increase Appeal, Make Better Design Decisions, and Teach through Design
William Lidwell, Kritina Holden, and Jill Butler

Content Strategy for the Web
Kristina Halvorson and Melissa Rach

Design Methods

Chapter 4 of this book provided descriptions and tips for the most common methods used in UX Design. However, the books in this list offer deeper and more comprehensive advice on design methods including research, design process, prototyping, and collaboration.

101 Design Methods: A Structured Approach for Driving Innovation in Your Organization
Vijay Kumar

Universal Methods of Design: 100 Ways to Research Complex Problems, Develop Innovative Ideas, and Design Effective Solutions
Bruce Hannington and Bella Martin

Prototyping: A Practitioner's Guide
Todd Zaki Warfel

Gamestorming: A Playbook for Innovators, Rulebreakers, and Changemakers
Dave Gray, Sunni Brown, and James Macanufo

Process

These books offer great advice for practicing designers on design mediums, communication, and working with product development teams in the software industry.

Sketching User Experiences: Getting the Design Right and the Right Design
Bill Buxton

Lean UX: Applying Lean Principles to Improve User Experience
Jeff Gothelf and Josh Seiden

Inspirational and Motivational

These books are just as the category suggests. They are intended to help motivate and inspire you during your journey to become a UX Designer as well as throughout your career.

Understanding Design: 175 Reflections on Being a Designer
Kees Dorst

Boundaries
Maya Lin

Creative Confidence: Unleashing the Creative Potential Within Us All
Tom Kelley and David Kelley

Mobile Design

These are good, easy reads to help you get started with designing for mobile products such as phones and tablets.

Mobile First
Luke Wroblewski

The Mobile Frontier: A Guide for Designing Mobile Experiences
Rachel Hinman

Acknowledgements

The authors would like to acknowledge all the wonderful people who supported us in making this book. A hearty thank you to Marianne Carmona, Karen Liu, Irina Tolstova, Dean Ashworth, and Yanyang Zhou for your early feedback, advice, and encouragement.

Thanks as well to Deb Aoki for permitting the use of her instructions and images for simple sketching and storyboarding in Chapter 4.

And a very special thanks to Matt Snyder for the long discussions and insights that helped us shape the character of this book. We cherish your mentorship.

Made in the USA
Middletown, DE
14 August 2018